So, What's the Deal?

by
Sharon Garrett

So, What's the Deal?

Published by S&G Publishing
Russellville, AR

Published in the United States of America

ISBN 978-0-9909430-0-6

To order additional copies of this resource, write to Believing God Ministries, P.O. Box 550, Russellville AR 72811; order online at www.BelievingGodMinistries.com

Printed in the United States of America

Acknowledgments

I want to give special thanks to Susan Brown and Elaine Hodges for a great job editing this study. Susan has been editing for ten years and currently works with published authors, churches, and other organizations. Elaine is an educator and has a passion for the English language. I really appreciate people that make me appear smarter than I am.

I also want to thank Ryan Taylor for the design and layout. I equally appreciate people that make my work appear prettier than I can. Ryan is 21-time national award winning graphic designer and video producer with over 15 years of professional experience. He owns F1rst Person Production in Russellville, AR and can be contacted through Facebook at www.facebook.com/f1rstpersonproductions.

I also want to thank my husband and children for their support and patience. It's not always easy to have a wife and a mother with her head stuck in a computer!

Contents

Contents

Contents

So, What's the Deal?

- INTRODUCTION -

I believe many people today have accepted Jesus as their Savior but do not understand what God expects of them. Usually their experience goes something like this: They receive salvation and, desiring to please God, begin trying to do the things they think will please God such as go to church, stop cursing, be honest, etc. After a while they find themselves in a vicious cycle of trying, failing, trying, failing; eventually they really do wear out. These precious believers get discouraged and slip back into old habits they are trying so hard to break. Looking around, they see all of the "good" people and think, "What is wrong with me? Why can't I get it right?" They feel something is missing but just don't know what it is. Not understanding God's plan and purpose is why many Christians lead the same lives as non-Christians with failing marriages, problems with their children, poor health, financial stress, etc. They have accepted Jesus as their Savior but have no idea what God wants from them beyond the salvation experience. They try to "be good," but when that doesn't work, they go back to their old lives and end up with all of the same problems they had before.

I spent a lot of years thinking things like, "Where's all the power, love, victory, and joy talked about in church? I see it in the Bible but not in my life. I'm glad I'm not going to hell, but what's the deal?" Dear sister, if you can relate to these sentiments at all, then keep reading, because the journey we are about to take together can change your life. It has certainly changed mine. There is a better way to live, and it's called the "Good News" for a reason! God, who truly is rich in loving-kindness and mercy, began an exciting work in me that has given me so many answers. I want to share these answers with you. I pray the Holy Spirit will breathe life into the words of this study and that you will never be the same!

WEEK ONE

MAIN CONCEPTS

DAY 1: AN INVITATION TO THE HOLY SPIRIT

DAY 2: MADE IN THE IMAGE OF GOD

DAY 3: A NEW WAY TO THINK

DAY 4: WHAT WE BELIEVE MATTERS

DAY 5: WE MUST CHOOSE LIFE

Day One

A First Priority

I want to begin by asking you to spend some time in prayer. Self-effort will never aid us in our quest to know Christ and live victorious Christian lives. The number one thing that will change you forever is a movement of the Holy Spirit within your heart. This is not a one time movement, but rather an ongoing movement that, hopefully, will last your entire life. If you are serious about wanting to live a life in the fullness of Christ, I am asking you to read the following scriptures and then write a prayer from your heart to God. You may want to refer back to this prayer at the beginning of each lesson or maybe in times of discouragement. The following scriptures may give you some ideas of what to write in your prayer.

[emphasis added]

Mark 8:25

> *"Once more Jesus put his hands on the man's eyes.* ***Then his eyes were opened, his sight was restored, and he saw everything clearly.****"*
>
> **Thought:** Although this scripture is referring to a physical healing, there are elements that can be applied to our spiritual eyes.

Acts 26:17-18

> *"I will rescue you from your own people and from the Gentiles. I am sending you to them 18 to open their eyes and turn them from darkness to light, and from the power of Satan to God, so that they may receive forgiveness* ***of sins and a place among those who are sanctified by faith in me****."*
>
> **Thought:** In this passage, Jesus, speaking to Paul, gives a clear picture of what He desires for us. We know that if we ask anything according to His will, it will be done (1John 5:14-15).

Matthew 13:15

> *"For this people's heart has become calloused; they hardly hear with their ears, and they have closed their eyes. Otherwise* ***they might see with their eyes, hear with their ears, understand with their hearts and turn, and I would heal them.****"*

Ephesians 1:17-19

> *"I keep asking that the God of our Lord Jesus Christ, the glorious Father, may* ***give you the Spirit of wisdom and revelation, so that you may know him better. 18 I pray also that the eyes of your heart may be enlightened in order that you may know the hope to which he has called you, the riches of his glorious inheritance in the saints, 19 and his incomparably great power for us who believe . . ."***

A possible prayer might be: "Dear Lord, thank You for loving me and desiring to have a relationship with me. Thank You for bringing this study into my life. I pray that through this study You will open my eyes and turn me from darkness to light. Please deliver me from the power of Satan and from blindness. Help me see with my eyes, hear with my ears, understand with my heart, and turn and be healed by You. Please give me the Spirit of wisdom and revelation so that I may know You better. I pray the eyes of my heart may be enlightened in order that I may know the hope to which You have called me, the riches of Your glorious inheritance, and Your incomparably great power for me. Lord, enable me to then share the Good News with others. Thank You, Father, in Christ's name I pray. Amen."

Record your own prayer.

____

____

____

____

____

____

____

____

____

____

____

____

____

____

____

Day Two

The Way We Work

In order for us to be able to live the life that Jesus has called us to, one of the first things we have to come to understand and believe is that God loves us just as we are. We don't have to change a thing about ourselves to make God love us; it's a done deal.

Read Romans 5:7-11 and record what it tells us about the way God feels about us before and after we are saved.

____

____

God loves us! God loves us! God loves us! Just as we are!!! Many of us have heard this since we were small, but few actually believe it. This is the reason that often, as soon as we get saved, we start in on our list to please God: "Don't drink, don't smoke, don't cuss, don't chew, and don't hang with those that do." God's message to us isn't, "I will accept you into My kingdom if you straighten up immediately," and nowhere in the Bible is this found. No, God's message is, "If you are sick, lonely, and in need of help, come to Me and let Me do a new thing within you, one you cannot do for yourself."

According to Philippians 1:6, who is going to accomplish a work within us?

____

____

Does this mean we have no part to play? Absolutely not! We are going to discover that there is nothing more challenging than fulfilling our role. But let me be clear on one point right from the beginning: our part is **NOT** to try really hard to stop sinning and make ourselves more pleasing to God. We will find that this is a fruitless effort and will not bring about victory in any sense of the word; rather, it results in more bondage.

To comprehend more fully what our role is in this relationship with God, we need to clearly understand the way we work. I want us to perceive, as much as possible, what makes up our created being both before and after salvation.

In Genesis 1:27 the Word tells us we are made in the image of God. "So God created man in his own image, in the image of God he created him…." God, as we know, is made up of three. Matthew 28:19 says, "Therefore go and make disciples of all nations, baptizing them in the name of the Father and of the Son and of the Holy Spirit . . . ." For the sake of explanation, let's say God looks like this.

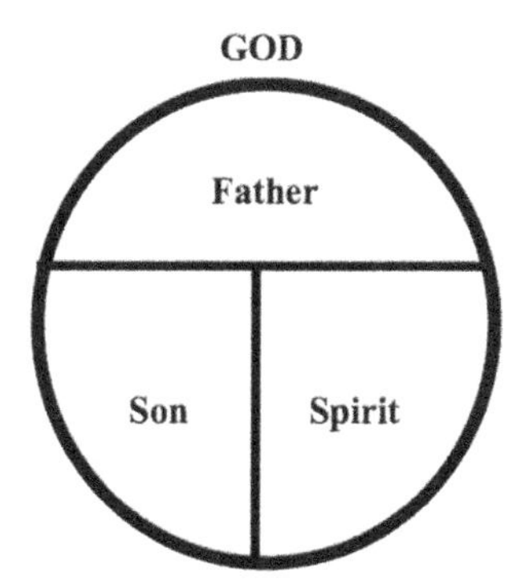

Of course, we are simplifying this. I'm sure we couldn't even comprehend the abstract dimensions of God, but for our purposes, we will keep it simple. As stated earlier, there is one God, but He is made up of three parts: Father, Son, and Spirit. The Father is the one who controls, has the plan, and is the source of everything. He is the Head. The Son is the Word of God and is the physical manifestation of God. He carries forth the will of God physically, so to speak. The Spirit is the part of God that empowers. He is the life-giving part of God. Now considering the fact that we were made in the image of God, let's say we look something like this:

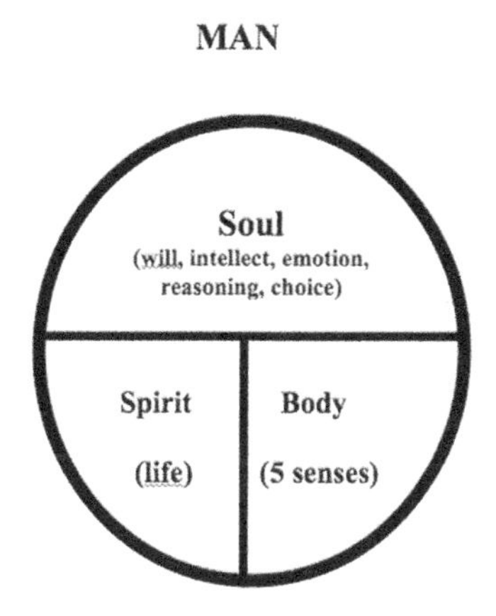

Just as God is one being, yet comprised of three parts, so we are one being made up of three parts. We each have a soul, a body, and a spirit.

Our souls are that part of us that receive and process data. They are where our wills exist, and it is through our souls (or our minds, if you will) that all choices are made. Our bodies are the part of us that carries forth the will of our minds. They can make no choices for themselves; they can only carry forth the commands of our minds. Our bodies, which represent the five senses, are the only part of us that are not eternal. Lastly, our spirits are that part of us that makes us living, eternal beings. Our spirits are where life abides.

Understanding that we are made of three parts and what each part does is vital to understanding many of the things we will be discussing throughout this study. Review what we have learned today, and get ready to learn other things about the way we work in the next lesson.

See you tomorrow!

Day Three

Renewing the Mind

In the last lesson, we learned that we are made in the image of God. Just as God is one God but comprised of the Father, Son, and Holy Spirit, so we are one being made up of a body, a soul, and a spirit. Having learned this, let's talk about the difference in the way we look before and after salvation.

Before we are saved, we receive information in one of two ways. Either we receive it from our bodies, or we receive it directly into our minds from an outside source.

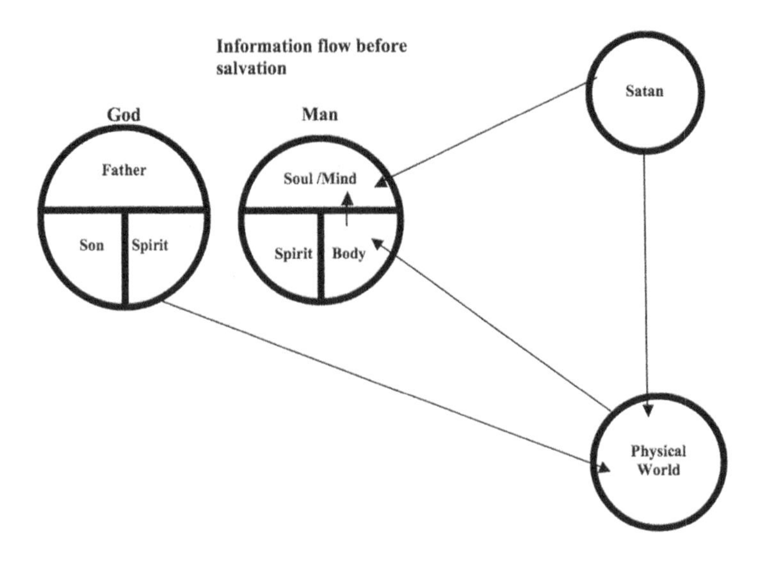

Before salvation, we learned to make our decisions by receiving information in our minds from (1) what our bodies told us through contact with the physical world, or (2) what Satan spoke into our minds. Through our intellects we would reason and come to decisions or make choices. We would send our choices to our bodies and our bodies would carry out our choices through actions. Our bodies are completely under the control of our minds. They can do nothing on their own. Once our souls and spirits depart, our bodies become lifeless heaps of material. When we are in a lost condition, we are separated from God and have no communion or fellowship with Him. However, once we become saved, we become new creations. This can be clearly seen in 2 Corinthians 5:17 which tells us, "Therefore, if anyone is in Christ, he is a new creation; the old has gone, the new has has come!" Again in Galatians 6:15 we are told, "Neither circumcision nor uncircumcision means anything; what counts is a new creation."

After salvation, we now look something like this:

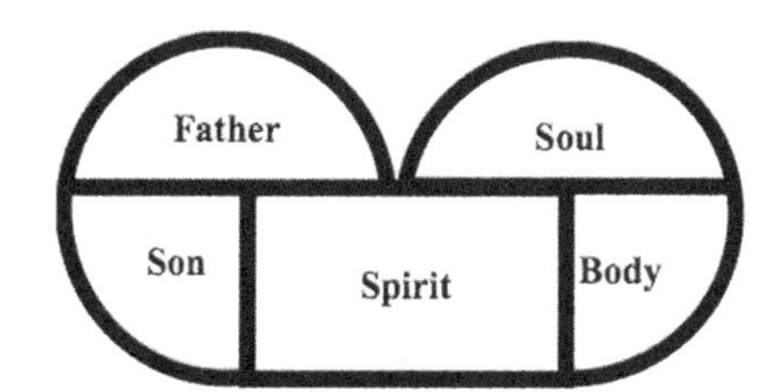

At salvation, the part of us that can fellowship or commune with God is born. This is called the new-birth and is where we get the term "born again." Our spirits become one with God's Spirit. In 1 Corinthians 6:17 it says, "But he who unites himself with the Lord is one with him in spirit." In 2 Corinthians 1:22, we are told that He "set his seal of ownership on us, and put his spirit in our hearts as a deposit, guaranteeing what is to come." Again in 1 John 4:13 we are told, "We know that we live in him and he in us, because he has given us of his Spirit." At the point of salvation, our spirits become one with the Spirit of God and automatically receive the very thoughts of God. We are told in 1 Corinthians 2:11, "For who among men knows the thoughts of a man except that man's spirit within him? In the same way no one knows the thoughts of God except the Spirit of God." Since God has given us His Spirit, uniting our spirits with His, our spirits actually have the very thoughts of God. Such is not the case for our minds. At salvation our minds have only obtained the **ability** to receive the very thoughts of God but do not automatically do so.

So, after salvation a new input channel into our mind is created. Our condition now looks something like this: (obviously not to scale)

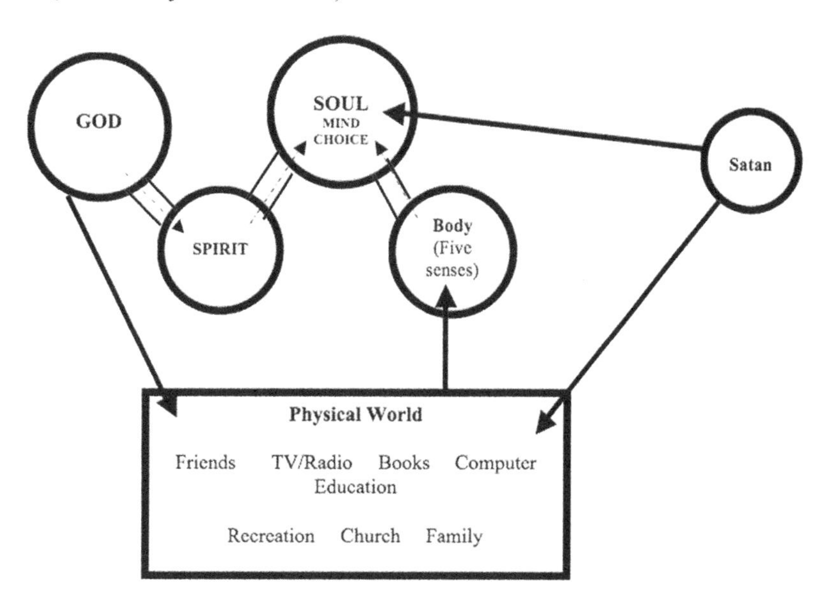

At the point of salvation our spirits are automatically one with God's, but our minds are in the same conditions they have always been in. The difference now is in our ability to receive from our spirits the very thoughts of God. Our minds don't automatically receive what our spirits are trying to tell us; they just have the *ability* to receive, whereas this wasn't even an option before salvation.

We have spent X number of years learning to make decisions in certain ways. Before we are saved we receive most of our information from our bodies or directly from Satan. Those channels are well used, well oiled, and running smoothly. Our minds have been trained to make decisions based on input from these channels. At the point of salvation, our minds don't automatically change but continue to operate under those same conditions. This is why the process of renewing our minds is so necessary. **Without renewal of our minds**, it is possible to be saved yet live totally defeated, miserable lives. This is why the battlefield of our lives is in our minds.

So, here we are, at the point of salvation: new spirits, darkened minds, and bodies waiting to do what they are told:

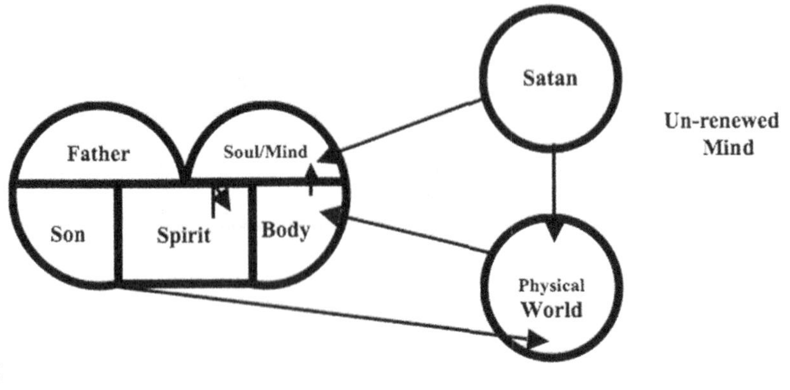

Here is where we **want** to be:

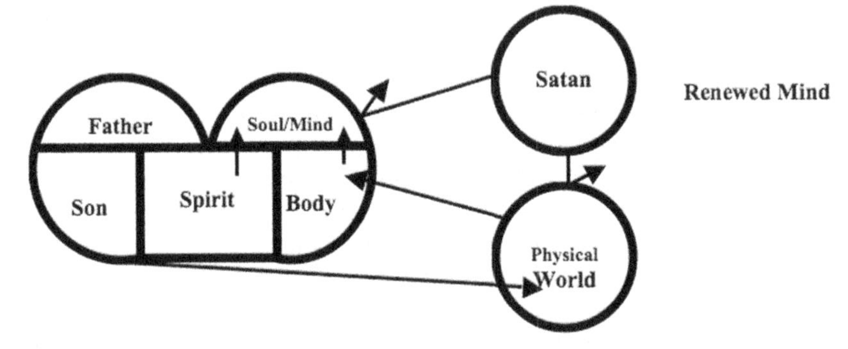

We want our spirits one with God's, giving our minds the very thoughts of God. The results: minds at peace, receiving all input from God, making choices in complete agreement with the instructions of God, telling our bodies what to do; bodies then carrying forth the will of God through our actions.

Truthfully, we are all somewhere between these two positions. It is in our minds that we play our part in our relationship with God.

What does Romans 12:2 tell us must happen in order for us to be able to know the will of God?

Ephesians 4:23 tells us we are "to be made new in the attitude of your minds." Just a few verses over, we are given a clue as to how that can happen. Read Ephesians 5:26-27 and list the way we can have our minds cleansed.

So, the question is, "If we aren't supposed to try really hard to do right and please God, then what is our part in the relationship? What is expected of us?" Our part in the pursuit of a relationship with God is simply to cooperate with the Holy Spirit in the process of renewing our minds. Although this sounds really simple and easy, nothing could be further from the truth. As you continue through this study, you may face some of the most difficult challenges of your life. You may find the quest to know God and what He expects of you to be the toughest thing you will ever embark on, but never stop, because **He is so worth it!**

As we close this lesson, I ask you to pray two things over the next few days. First, ask the Lord to grant you the grace to believe that He really does love you. Secondly, ask the Lord to grant you the grace to never stop pressing into Him, regardless of how difficult the journey might become.

Until we come together again, may God bless you with abundant mercy and grace, and may He stir such a desire in your heart to know Him that nothing short of face to face will ever cause your pursuit of Him to end. Praise His name!!

Day Four

The Importance of What We Think/Believe

In our last lesson, we learned the basic way we work spiritually. We learned that our part in pursuing a relationship with God is to allow God to do His work in us and to get into agreement with Him in every area of our lives. This is the process of renewing our minds. If we want to live an abundant life in Christ, we need to allow the Holy Spirit to enlighten our minds to God's way of thinking. He wants to, is waiting to. As we seek to know God, we must realize that life is a series of choices. We must decide whose voice we are going to believe and adhere to in making those choices, God's or Satan's. Unless we actively choose God's way of thinking, we will automatically choose Satan's.

God has a plan He has set forth in His Word and by His Spirit. His plan will lead to a victorious life for anyone who is willing to find and follow it. It is available to "anyone that will." **Our part is to choose to put our confidence in what He tells us.** We really have to understand that to walk out of our problems, bondages, insecurities, fears, and anything else that is holding us back, we must adjust our thinking. Life is lived in the mind. What we think and believe affects everything in our lives.

Read the following passages of scripture and record what they have to say about our thinking. List any insights you receive regarding the importance of what we think and the possible ways our thinking might affect us.

Romans 1:21 ____

____

1 Corinthians 14:20 ____

____

Ephesians 4:17 ____

____

Philippians 4:8 ____

____

2 Peter 3:1 ____

____

In each of these scriptures, notice the author, under the leadership of the Holy Spirit, did not address the action but the thinking. This is because all action is preceded by thought. What we think or believe always dictates the choices we make. The choices we make always dictate the condition or situation we end up with. Let me repeat for emphasis.

THE WAY WE THINK/ WHAT WE BELIEVE

DETERMINES

CHOICES/DECISIONS WE MAKE

DETERMINE

CURRENT CONDITION/ SITUATION

When we really grasp the truth of this, we begin to see how important it is to believe and think according to truth. When, through the power of the Holy Spirit, we begin to grasp this, we will become much more serious about what we choose to believe. What we believe really does matter.

God has a good plan for us; it will lead us to a purpose-filled life of joy and power. Satan also has a plan for us. Although he can make his way look very inviting, it will ultimately lead to disappointment and destruction. If what we believe is the basis of all our choices, it stands to reason that both God and Satan want to influence what we believe. There is a battle going on for our minds, and our part is to decide whom we are going to listen to and believe.

Each of us has a system of beliefs that has formed who and what we are. Some of the things we believe are true, and some of the things we believe are not. How can we know which is which? There is only one way to know for certain, and that is to closely examine our beliefs to see if they agree with what God says. Nothing but God's Word can be used as a measuring stick, because it is the only infallible thing with which we have to compare. Everything else is changeable. We certainly can't let our feelings be our guide; they're as fickle as Arkansas weather. Really, the only absolute we have is the Word of God.

Look at Matthew 24:35 and write it on the following lines.

____

____

God's Word is absolute truth, both now and forever. Therefore, if we want to be able to make accurate judgments about the things we believe, we must align our judgments with His Word. If we want to experience the life God has for us, we must be willing to let go of any belief that is contrary to what God says in His Word.

If we make decisions according to the way we feel, what we want, etc., without regard to what God says, we will walk in defeat. Often, we don't see that the way we think about things every day dictates what we become, but it does.

In our lives we constantly make choices. Choices made based on what we think, feel, want or don't want, etc. are decisions based on our flesh. However, choices made based on what God says in His Word and in our spirits through the Holy Spirit are decisions made according to the Spirit.

Read the following scriptures and fill in the blanks.

John 6:63, "The ________________ gives ________________;

the ________________ counts for ______________________."

John 3:6, "____________________ gives birth to _________________,

but ________________ gives birth to _____________________."

Every choice made in accordance with the flesh will lead us to defeat in the end.

Every choice made in accordance with the Spirit will ultimately lead to victory.

Generally no one decision will make or break our lives, with exceptions, such as driving drunk. However, choices made repeatedly, day after day, lead us to our present situations.

We must learn to make our decisions based on the "Spirit" not the "flesh."

Let's end this lesson by asking the Father to enable us to make decisions according to His Spirit. In the next lesson, we will look at a practical example of what we have learned today.

Day Five

The Importance of Choice

In the last lesson, we learned that what we believe determines the choices we make which determine our current conditions or situations. We also learned that decisions made in accordance with the flesh will lead to defeat, while choices made in agreement with the Spirit lead to life and victory. The daily choices we make determine the direction of our lives. Today, let's apply this principle to an everyday, real life example so that we might better understand what we have been learning. See if you can identify with anything in the following scenario.

Suppose you don't sleep very well one night which causes you to get up late the next morning. You jump out of bed and start rushing around trying to get yourself and the kids ready for the day. While you are trying to get breakfast, one of your kids says, "Mom, I forgot that today is school picture day." You rush to the closet looking for the outfit you specifically bought for picture taking, only to find it is in the piles of laundry you haven't yet had a chance to do. As you hurry into the kitchen to tell the kids to stop fighting and quickly finish eating, your husband says, "Babe, I've asked you a hundred times to clean the table in the computer room so I can work on my guitar. Do you think you might get it done any time soon?"

At this point you could choose to do any of the following things:

A. Blow your stack and scream at the kids to shut up. Tell your husband exactly what he can do with his guitar, **(flesh)**

B. Walk calmly out of the room, go into the bathroom, and scream silently to yourself, **(better flesh)**, or

C. Pray, "God, everything in me feels like I'm about to explode, but Your word tells me to endure all things with peace and rejoicing. Nothing in me feels like doing this. Please give me the ability to line up with Your Word." **(Spirit)**

God is faithful; He will help you. You may be able to stop and realize that even if you missed a day at work or your kids made it to school an hour late, it's not that big of a deal.

You see, Satan understands the principle at work here better than we do. He knows that if we make our decisions in the flesh, he can accomplish his purposes in our lives; therefore, he cranks up the pressure. God is a God of peace. How much better would this situation be if the minute we woke up late we prayed and asked God to help us do the impossible?

Other examples we could discuss might be choices we face when:

A. Someone says something hurtful to or about us.
B. We have to choose between Bible reading and a movie or a good book.
C. We have to decide whether to clean the house, go shopping, or talk on the phone.
D. Someone tells us a piece of juicy gossip.

The list could go on and on. Making choices based on God's Word instead of the flesh may sound easy, but I don't think there is anything as hard as saying no to our emotions and feelings and praying instead. In the moment, it feels so much better to give in to the flesh than it does to the Spirit. The flesh is instant gratification, but the Spirit is extended victory and abundant life. The one thing it usually is not is instant relief.

Let's say that in the above situation you failed miserably and totally blew up at your family. Does that one instance mean your life is going to be a miserable failure? Of course not. **It's not the one decision made in accordance with the flesh that destroys us; it's the mind that is not trained to habitually disregard the flesh and exalt God's Word that brings about a life of failure.** Usually one bad decision leads to another and another and another. Let's continue with our example by extending it through the rest of the day. Let's say that after you blew up at everyone, you get the kids off to school. While driving to work, you begin to cool off and realize you left on bad terms with every member of your family. You feel really guilty and arrive at work with a dark cloud hanging over you. When a friend comes by to gossip about someone, you jump right on board with it because you already have an ugly, unhappy heart. This only adds to the big, dark cloud already hovering over you.

Generally, you will make a series of bad choices all day. By the time you crawl into bed that night, you are going to feel horrible about yourself and pray that tomorrow will be a better day.

You see, at the given moment, it doesn't seem that important to make a choice in accordance with God's Word, but it has a greater effect upon our lives than we realize. **No, it's not the one time we ignore the Spirit and give into the flesh that causes us to live in bondage; it's the lifestyle of it.** Many of us are living according to our own desires, how we feel, etc., but we still want the fruits of the Spirit to manifest in our lives. It will never happen that way.

There are 10,000 different situations we could discuss, but the principle is always the same. Decisions made in accordance with the flesh lead to destruction, while decisions made in accordance with the Spirit lead to life.

All of us have ideas about what we want or need for happiness and a fulfilling life. We make choices daily hoping to obtain what it is we think we need, but **only one thing is needed.**

Read Matthew 6:33 and write exactly what that one thing is according to the Word of God.

____

____

Yes, all we really need is to seek God and His kingdom first, and everything else will be added to us. We see this in God's Word, but somehow we don't truly believe it. We don't train our minds to think this way, so we spend most of our time striving for what we think will make us happy, never obtaining what we are looking for. It is lining up with God's Word, situation by situation, that leads us to an overall life condition of victory. Each of us, in a general sense, says we want to line up with God's Word, but in the minute by minute decisions, we line up more often than not with what we want and feel, not what God says. This is the reason many of us are in bondage, living with all kinds of problems, unhappiness, and defeat.

The bottom line is this: Are we willing to believe and trust God in the details? Are we willing to trust God and take His Word literally? If not, we will continue in the futility of our thinking and make choices leading to bondage and destruction.

Trying to hold on to our own ways and what seems right to us, and refusing to conform our thinking to God's, cheats us of the abundant life that God so desires for us to have.

What does Matthew 16:24 tell us we must do if we want to follow Jesus?

____

____

John 12:25 has a similar theme. What does it say?

____

____

These verses are referring to the lordship of our lives, which includes the way we make decisions and the way we choose to think. Are we going to be the lord of our lives or is God? We need to determine in our hearts that we want to think in accordance with God's Word, then earnestly pray for the Lord to do a work in our minds that will enable us to carry this decision through. **God has to do it,** but we have to want it. Oh, how I pray God will open the eyes of our hearts to know, understand, and seek after a life of being in agreement with His Word.

WEEK TWO

MAIN CONCEPTS

DAY 1: WHAT ARE STRONGHOLDS

DAY 2: HOW WE OVERCOME STRONGHOLDS

DAY 3: UNDERSTANDING OUR TRUE CONDITION STEP BY STEP

DAY 4: UNDERSTANDING THE NEED TO TAKE RESPONSIBILITY

DAY 5: RESPONDING TO LIFE IN AGREEMENT WITH GOD

Day One

Strongholds

During this week of study, one of the things we will discuss is strongholds . . . what they are, how they affect us, and what we can do about them. To begin, I want to draw your attention back to a statement I made in the previous week's study, which was that each of us has a system of beliefs that has formed who and what we are. Our belief system is basically the way we think and have developed primarily from what we have been taught and have experienced. It is in this belief system that we will find strongholds.

Although our overall belief systems may vary, we all share common areas of belief. For example, we all have beliefs about God, ourselves, our government, our relationships, our worth, and so on. In other words, we don't all have the same beliefs about things, but we all have beliefs about the same things. For the remainder of this study, we are going to examine key areas of our belief systems in the light of God's Word. We will discuss the area of belief, then look and see what the Word says about that subject. Then, we can individually examine our thinking regarding that area and determine whether we are in agreement with God. Where we see discrepancies, we can make adjustments to our beliefs and begin to line our thinking up with God's. This is the process of renewing our minds and is a must if we want to live in the victory of Jesus Christ.

In beginning this process of examining our beliefs, it is very important to become aware of strongholds, understand what strongholds are, and realize they can keep us from being able to see and receive truth in a given area of our thinking. Remember, our desire is to pursue a belief system that is in total agreement with God's Word.

Having said all of that, let's get started. What is a stronghold? According to the American Heritage Dictionary, a stronghold is:

> "A fortified place or a fortress. A place of survival or refuge. An area dominated or occupied by a special group or distinguished by a special quality: a stronghold of democracy."

It is basically an area where something or someone is safe to "carry on." Throughout scripture we see the term used to indicate a place where one went to remain safe during a battle or a season of war. Therefore, when I am talking about a stronghold in our minds, I'm referring to an area in our belief system or thinking in which Satan has built himself a place to carry on. It is an area where we are **deceived**, and the enemy is **safe** to carry out his plans in our lives.

Satan has a definite plan for our lives, and he knows if he can control our thinking, he can control us. Read the following passages of scripture and then answer the questions.

1 Peter 5:8

What is your enemy the devil doing?

____

____

2 Corinthians 2:11, Ephesians 6:11, 1 Timothy 3:7, 2 Timothy 2:26

According to these verses, does Satan have a will? Yes _____ No _____

According to 2 Timothy 2:26, what does Satan have to do first, in order to get us to do his will?

____

Based on the authority of the Word, is the following statement true or false?

> Satan has a will and he schemes, plans, and lays traps for us in order to get us to accomplish his will. True ______ False ______

John 8:44, 2 Corinthians 11:14

Can Satan act good? Yes ____ No ____

Who is the father of lies? _________________

Since what we think leads to the decisions we make, we had better believe that Satan wants to influence our thinking. Satan works wrong thinking patterns into our minds. If he can get us to believe lies, then we will fulfill his purposes through the choices we make. If we believe a lie, then to us it is true and often will bring the same result as if the lie actually were true. Remember, what we believe determines the choices we make, which determine what we end up with. So, Satan tries to build strongholds in our minds - patterns of thinking (or beliefs) that are not true but become so ingrained in us that we put our faith or confidence in what they tell us and act accordingly.

For example: Let's say you are very beautiful, but Satan has convinced you that you are ugly. What's the good of being beautiful if you think you are ugly? Your beauty will not benefit you because all of your actions and decisions will be made based on the belief that you are ugly. Therefore, you will actually live the life of an ugly person even though you are beautiful.

This is an example of exactly how Satan steals from us. Many times Satan begins early in our lives putting lies into our thoughts. We think they are our thoughts, but they are not. Over time he whispers them into our minds enough that we begin to put our faith in them. We believe these lies and make choices based on our beliefs, just like in the example above. I know a girl who is very attractive and has a perfect body. But she thinks she is ugly and her personal care of herself reflects this mindset. "Why bother," she says. How sad! This type of thinking is the result of a stronghold, a belief that something is true when in fact it is not. Strongholds never line up with God's Word because they are of Satan. They always bring about Satan's purposes in our lives. They don't lift us up; rather, they tear us down and are directly opposed to the will of God.

Until God has completed His work in us, we each have certain strongholds Satan has built in our minds that we are comfortable with and will quickly run to in times of trouble. They go beyond wrong thinking and become areas of enslavement. We strongly believe these things and often will get very defensive if these particular beliefs are challenged. Strongholds always lead to bondage. In any area that we have a stronghold, know there is a related area of bondage. Here are examples of some common strongholds:

1. __________ is the reason I am this way.
2. I'm not as good as everyone else.
3. I'm ugly, dumb, etc.
4. I can't __________.
5. ______ will never change.
6. I have to do _______ because _________.
7. __________ is wrong with me.

The possible strongholds that could be listed are as varied as the number of people walking the earth. We must understand that strongholds are real, that they are the enemy's area of safety in our lives, and their sole purpose is to steal victorious living.

As we go through the different areas of our belief system, be alert to those things that cause you to become agitated. If we are discussing a particular belief, and you can see in the Word that your thinking in that area doesn't agree with God, you should have the attitude of "Lord, change me!" If you don't and begin to argue or get angry, there is a very strong possibility that Satan has a stronghold in that area of your belief system. You can bet he will fight to keep it.

Let's close this lesson with a prayer.

> "Dear Father in Heaven, please give us the grace to face areas of our thinking that do not line up with Your Word. Enable us to see the truth and embrace it wholeheartedly. Father, Your Word is truth and all Your ways are right! In any area where what we believe does not agree with You, we are wrong and we acknowledge this before You. Thank You for Your Word, Your truth, and Your Life. In Christ's name we come before you and place our plea. Amen!"

Day Two

Overcoming Strongholds

In Day One of this week's study, we defined a stronghold as an area in our belief system or thinking in which Satan has built himself a place to carry on. It is an area where we are deceived, and the enemy is safe to carry out his plans in our lives. We learned that strongholds don't lift us up; rather, they tear us down and are directly opposed to the will of God. We talked about the importance of being watchful for strongholds as we examine the different areas of our belief system.

Having defined strongholds, let's turn our attention to how we overcome them and recapture those areas of our thinking. Following is a list of five basic things we can do to break free in any area of our thinking that doesn't line up with the Word of God.

1. **We must recognize where we have a stronghold**. We have to ask God to reveal to us any stronghold Satan has built in our minds. Then we need to begin to examine certain patterns of behavior in our lives. Anywhere that we are living in consistent defeat represents an area of our thinking that isn't in agreement with God and can indicate a possible stronghold. I want to warn you, however, that we ourselves are not smart enough to identify our strongholds; it takes revelation from God. We must ask Him to reveal any area of our thinking that is a stronghold of the enemy. He is faithful and will do so. Remember, He wants to show us because He wants us to get into agreement with Him and live in freedom.

2. **We must determine to make God's Word the absolute authority in our lives.** When our thinking doesn't agree with what we see in the Word, we have to throw out our thinking and exalt God's Word instead. We must ask God to help us to do this. Our prayer might be something like, "God, everything in me right now feels like . . . , but I know your Word says . . . . Please do a supernatural work in me to enable me to obey your Word."

3. **We must spend time in the Word.** We cannot know what God's Word says if we don't spend time reading it. If we are not reading and studying the Bible daily and asking God to open the eyes of our hearts and minds to understand His Word, then how will we know if our thoughts are in agreement? Spend time in the Word!!

4. **We need to make a habit of finding something for which to praise God.** When we use our minds to praise and worship God, we exalt Him, and Satan has more difficulty operating in our minds. When we are trying to break an old pattern of thinking and get into agreement with God, praising God will weaken the enemy's influence over our minds. This is not always easy to do, especially if our stronghold is of a complaining or negative nature. However, if we will start looking for a reason to praise God, praise will grow in our lives. We must ask God to help us have thankful hearts. He will do a work in us if we will begin making the choice to praise Him.

5. **We must learn to turn quickly to prayer because God is our source for everything.** God is looking for someone who is actively pursuing His will. Girls, if we are asking for His help and trying to obey Him, we can absolutely know He is listening to our prayer and will help us! We can trust Him; He will defeat the enemy in our lives. He hears our prayers!!

Read the following scriptures and record the promise and the condition (where applicable) found in the passage. I did the first one for you as an example.

Psalms 34:15

If I am righteous, the eyes of the Lord are on me, and His ears are attentive to my cry.

Note: Just in case you are like me and the first thought you have is "but I don't think I'm all that righteous," let me remind you that our righteousness comes through faith in Jesus, Romans 3:22.

Psalms 14:2

____

____

Mark 11:22-23

____

____

2 Chronicles 16:9

____

____

God is on our side. He will do wonderful and mighty things for us, but we must cooperate with Him. We do this by getting into agreement with Him. He will help us overcome all of the areas of bondage in our lives, for nothing is impossible for Him. There is no stronghold of the enemy in our lives that God cannot overcome, but we have to actively agree with Him in order for this to be accomplished. God promises us in His Word that we can and will overcome the enemy. Read each of the following verses and record what it promises.

Luke 10:19

____

____

John 16:33

____

____

1 John 5:4-5

____

____

Romans 8:37

____

____

Dear sisters, Satan wants to keep us blinded so that he can continue to have a safe place to operate in our minds. God wants us to be free! We have a choice. We can continue to hang on to beliefs that steal our freedom, or we can begin right now to choose to agree with God and go free. With my whole heart, I pray we will choose the latter. It's not easy, but freedom is so worth the effort. As this lesson closes, I ask you to pray for God to enlighten your mind and strengthen your heart to learn the truth of His Word and get into agreement with it. This is my prayer for you!

Day Three

Recognize Our True Condition

As mentioned previously, for the remainder of our study we are going to discuss key areas we each have in our belief systems. I made the statement, "We don't all have the same beliefs about things, but we all have beliefs about the same things." We are going to begin examining these areas in the light of God's Word. Hopefully, anywhere we find a discrepancy between our beliefs and what we see in the Word, we will make the necessary adjustments in our thinking, which will result in more and more freedom.

The first area of belief I want us to examine is what I'm going to call the area of "Responsibility of Condition." Each of us is currently in a certain life situation and operating in a certain way. We are living in unique and varied circumstances. This life situation, these circumstances, and our particular way of doing things define who and what we are. I'm going to refer to this state of being as our "condition." Some of us may be very content with our current condition; others may be content but feel the need for improvement, and still others may be completely dissatisfied. Regardless of which of these particular descriptions fits you, the point is each of us owns a condition.

One of the first steps we must take in order to move forward in Christ is to recognize our true condition. We all have beliefs about ourselves, some true and some not true. The beliefs that are false are what I want to pick on for a moment. There are several examples in the Word in which a person or people believed something about themselves that wasn't true. I picked two for us to look at.

Read Revelation 3:1 and answer the following questions.

What did the church of Sardis have a reputation of and in all likelihood believed about

themselves? ____

What was the truth about the church from God's point of view?

____

Which was the actual truth? ____

The church of Sardis thought they were alive with all kinds of works as proof, but the truth was, they were dead. They were going to reap the benefits of their actual condition, not what they thought about themselves. It is the same for us. Our condition will reflect the truth of what we are, not what we think we are. I might believe I am eating right, but if I'm fifty pounds overweight, the truth is, I'm not eating right. My condition reflects the actual truth.

Another example of this same blindness can be seen in 1 Corinthians 4:8.

What did the church at Corinth obviously believe about themselves?

____

In examining Paul's comment, was this the truth? ______________________

When we operate in anything other than the truth in any area, we are in bondage. Unless the Holy Spirit reveals these areas of blindness to us, we will not see them. If we do not want to walk in spiritual blindness, it is imperative that we begin to seek to know our true condition. No spiritual progress can be made without first coming to grips with the truth about ourselves. Take salvation, for example. Before we can be saved, we must first come to the realization we are sinners, unable to save ourselves, and in need of a Savior. This is ascertaining our true condition. In the same way, until we discern the truth about any given area of our lives, we cannot make the appropriate changes that are necessary.

I want to clarify that we are never going to be able to assess our **total** true condition all at one time; it would be too overwhelming. However, through revelation from the Holy Spirit, we can ascertain our true condition in a step-by-step process. We may not be able to comprehend the complete truth of our condition, but we can come into the knowledge of our true condition area by area. As the Spirit reveals things to us, we can make general assessments of "I am not happy" or "I'm not living in victory." We can also make specific assessments, such as "I am in financial disaster," "My marriage is failing," "I'm overweight," "I am too impatient with my kids," and so on.

The point I am trying to make is that no change will ever occur in any situation, circumstance, or condition until we first comprehend the truth about it.

Read John 8:32. In this verse, what are we told will set us free? __________________.

That is right, knowing the truth. It's the very first step in our quest to walk into the life Christ wants us to live. We will never glean the truth in and of ourselves; we must ask God to reveal it to us. He is faithful and will do it.

Now, I have a question to ask you. Is knowing the truth all we need in order to walk into freedom? No, it is not. I might know the truth that I am an alcoholic, but that in itself will not enable me to be set free from the bondage of alcoholism. This leads to the next step we must take if we want to change our condition.

In order to live a better life full of blessing, peace, joy, and power, we must not only recognize our true condition, but must take full responsibility for it. We have to face the fact that it's not someone else's fault that we are in whatever condition we find ourselves. We are responsible for where we are.

Now, before you get mad and stop reading, hear me out. You may be saying, "You have no idea what has happened to me that has caused me to be this way." You are right. I have no personal knowledge of your life, but regardless of what has happened to you, it isn't why you are in your present situation and condition. Your response to what has happened to you has brought you to this point. What you believe about what has been brought to you has formed your current condition.

If we believe it is someone or something else's fault that we are the way we are or are in the circumstance we are in, then we will also believe we are helpless to do anything about our situations. We will believe our situations can only be changed if something outside of ourselves change. We will live as victims instead of victors.

I know many bad things happen to people, and I'm not saying these misfortunes do not affect us. But it is important to understand that although many things may affect us, they should not become the **determining factors** of our lives. Often something bad happens to someone, and that bad experience defines that person's life from that point on. For example, let's say a young woman marries an abusive man who is selfish, demeaning, hateful, and just downright mean. After years of abuse, the unhappy marriage comes to an end. Once free from this horrible relationship, the woman becomes a man hater, refuses to ever marry again, starts a career, and never allows herself to become close to another man. As she grows older, she becomes more and more bitter and talks degradingly about men every chance she gets. Although what happened to her was sad, wrong, and unfair, that experience did not mold her into what she became; rather, it was her response to that experience that formed her. We have all seen examples of this exact scenario.

It is true that many people allow a bad event or series of events to define their entire lives. Yet think about this truth for a moment: If bad events or experiences determine what we become, then everyone faced with similar circumstances will be equally affected and react the same way. They will each end up in the same condition. We know this isn't the case.

Allow me to share a real life example with you: My grandmother had five children and was living a normal, picturesque life. Her husband was an electrician and made a good living. When he was forty years old and their children ranged in age from teenage to four years, he had a stroke. His mentality was that of a two-year-old for several years, and he never worked again. He lived twenty years after this occurred. This was before the age of disability income, so my grandmother had to go to work, raise five children, and take care of an invalid husband. They were impoverished and life was very hard for her. Other heartbreaking things occurred in her life. Her oldest son was molested and later killed himself. By anyone's definition, my grandmother had a very difficult life with much heartbreak. But to hear her tell it, she had a wonderful life and felt that God had been so good to her. She was one of the happiest people I have ever known. I can honestly say that I never, not one time, heard her complain about anything, and I spent a lot of time with her.

On the other hand, I know people that have had nothing horrible or especially hard ever happen to them; yet they are negative, bitter, and hateful people. You see, it really isn't what happens to us that forms who and what we are; it is what we choose to do with our experiences that dictates what our lives become.

I know this is a really hard truth to accept. If you have spent a lot of time blaming others or an experience for where you are and what you have become, then this is going to make you angry. But I ask you to remember what we talked about in the last two lessons. If your reaction to what I am saying is anger, you may have a stronghold in this area of your thinking. Please remember, a stronghold is an area where Satan has established a safe place to carry out his will for your life. Please seek the Father for the grace to deal with this issue. He loves you and He will gently lead you into a new way of thinking about what has happened in your past.

In the next lesson, we will examine several examples in scripture of this principle in action. May God's grace surround and support us until we come together again.

Day Four

Take Responsibility for Yourself

In the last lesson, we discussed the importance of understanding our true condition. We will never be able to assess our total true condition all at one time, but through revelation from the Spirit, we can ascertain our true condition in a step-by-step process. We talked about the importance of taking responsibility for our condition. It is not what is brought to us that determines the outcome of our lives; rather, our responses to our experiences dictate what we become. Unless we are willing to take responsibility for ourselves, we will have a "victim" mentality, believing we cannot change unless our situation or circumstances change. Although it may be difficult to accept this, only in doing so are we empowered to overcome.

I never want you to take my word about something without examining it in the light of God's Word, so get ready to do some work. We are going to look at several examples in scripture of this principle in action. I am going to ask you to read a lot of passages, and when we are finished, I believe you are going to see the truth of this principle in scripture. I am going to walk you through the lives of several people in the Bible. By comparing and contrasting, we are going to see that each person we study had troubles, fear, disappointment, or just plain old bad stuff happen to them. Yet it wasn't what was brought to them that determined where they ended up. It was their response to what was brought.

The first situation I want us to study is going to be found in Genesis chapters 37-50. If you are extremely zealous, I want to encourage you to read from Genesis chapter 37 all the way through Genesis chapter 50. However, if you do not have the time for that, then following are selected verses you can read to get a general idea of what happened in the lives of the people we are studying.

Read the following verses and then fill in the chart provided.

Genesis 37, Genesis 39, Genesis 41:1, Genesis 41:8-16, Genesis 41:25, Genesis 41:28, Genesis 41:38-45, Genesis 42:1-6, and Genesis 50:19-21

	Joseph	**Josephs Brother's**
1. What unfortunate situation was brought into the life (lives) of the characters indicated?		
2. How did the character(s) respond to the situation(s) he (they) faced?		
3. What was the result of the character's response?		

In these passages we read that Joseph and his brothers were dealt some injustices. First Jacob (Israel) loved Joseph more than he loved his other children. This isn't right or fair, and in those days it was more than just an emotional slight. Joseph could have very well inherited the rights culturally due his oldest brother. Next, we saw that Joseph tattled on his brothers and got them into trouble, another unpleasant thing that they had to deal with. We then read that Joseph was sold by his brothers as a slave to the Ishmaelites and taken to Egypt where he was sold again to Potiphar. Potiphar's wife propositioned Joseph, and when he turned her down, she falsely accused him of sexual advances for which he was thrown into prison. While in prison he was forgotten by the cupbearer to whom he had shown kindness. All of these things were injustices of a magnitude that would be hard for us to comprehend. So, in this example, we have individuals faced with adversities that were not of their choice . . . misfortunes that could make them bitter.

Now let's examine each party's response to what happened to them. First, Joseph's brothers allowed their father's indiscretions and Joseph's attitude and lack of humility to cause them to become jealous and angry. They grew bitter to the point they wanted to kill Joseph. They tried to solve their problems based on how they felt and what they thought instead of what was right and true. They sinned against their brother. They, in effect, stole his inheritance and lied to their father. Joseph, on the other hand, trusted in God. He allowed God to do a work in his heart. He did what was right even to his own detriment. Unlike his brothers, he didn't try to make things happen for himself and solve his own problems; he waited on God. He continued to do right even when nothing was going his way.

Lastly, let's discuss the result of each response. In what condition did Joseph's brothers end up? They ended up nearly starving to death along with their families. It must have been extremely uncomfortable having to admit to their father what they had done. Thinking to exalt themselves over Joseph, they became his servants and were completely at Joseph's mercy for the welfare of their entire families for the rest of their lives. They actually ended up with the very thing they were trying so hard to avoid. On the other hand, Joseph, who was handed the greater injustice by far, ended up with everything. He was rich, powerful, strong, and gained the blessing of his father. He had a wife and children. Most of all, we are told, God was with him, and he was blessed beyond measure. Can you see that it wasn't what happened to these people that caused the condition they ended up with? It was their response to what happened that was the determining factor.

Let's look at another comparison. Read the following verses and fill in the chart provided on the next page.

Numbers 13:1-2, Numbers 13:16-32, Numbers 14:20-24, Numbers 14:36-38, Deuteronomy 1:35-36, Joshua 14:6-15

	Caleb and Joshua	**The Other Spies**
1. What challenge was set before each of these men?		
2. How did they respond to the challenge?		
3. What were the results of their responses?		

In this situation, twelve men were all faced with the exact same challenge . . . to spy out the land of their enemies. When they went into the land of Canaan, all twelve saw and experienced the exact same thing: a land of bounty inhabited by giants. Two of the men responded with faith in God's ability to be true to His Word. The others responded without faith in God and His Word. Joshua and Caleb lived to see the Word of the Lord fulfilled; the others died in their poverty. They were all given the exact same challenge, but it wasn't the challenge that dictated their outcome; it was their response to the challenge.

Girls, it really is our response to things that makes or breaks our lives. When we respond to challenges with faith in God and His Word, we will be victorious. When we don't, we will be defeated. "Oh, Lord, please enable us to deal with the things we face by trusting You to do what You say You will!"

Next time we will look at one other example! See you then!

Day Five

A Call to Action

If we want to move into the victorious life to which we have been called, we must understand our true condition, take responsibility for it, and choose to address it in the truth of God's Word. In the last lesson, we looked at two scenarios in scripture which illustrate these principles in action. Let's finish the week by looking at one final scriptural example of what we have been talking about.

This example is found in the stories of two interesting women. Read the following scriptures and fill in the chart provided.

Ruth 1:1-8, Ruth 1:16-19, Ruth 2:1-13, Ruth 4:13-16, 2 Samuel 13:1-20

	Ruth	**Tamar**
1. What unfortunate situation was brought into the life of the character indicated?		
2. How did the character respond to the situation faced?		
3. What was the result of the character's response?		

Once again we have two people who had a bad experience. Ruth lost her husband. If a woman lost her husband in those days, she either had to remarry, have a son old enough to care for her, or go back to her father's home. Ruth didn't have any children at the time of her husband's death; when he died, she basically lost her entire life. She chose to go with Naomi to a strange land and build a new life with her mother-in-law. She chose to serve her mother-in-law's God. Ruth was a nobody, a foreigner, but because of her attitude and her character, she ended up marrying a very rich man and had a son. She became the great, great grandmother of King David. In contrast to this, look at Tamar. Tamar was the daughter of the king. She had beauty, culture, possessions, and social status. She was raped by her brother and greatly shamed. We are told that she lived the rest of her life in her brother's home, a desolate woman. Therefore, she allowed one horrible experience to rob her of the rest of her life. Both of these women were handed a huge injustice. However, it wasn't the injustice that determined their future; it was, once again, their response to it.

We could look at many other contrasting stories in the Word: David vs. Saul, Samuel vs. Eli, Abigail vs. Michal, Elisha vs. Gehazi, the eleven disciples vs. Judas, and many others. All of these stories point to the same principle: it is not what is brought to individuals that dictate what they become; it is their response to what is brought that is the determining factor. The absolute truth is, we are totally responsible for what we are and what we become. If we are willing to face the fact that the way we think about what has happened to us has led us to the decisions we have made in our lives, then we are empowering ourselves to be able to make the necessary changes to turn our situations and lives around. As I stated earlier, if we continue to blame something or someone outside of ourselves for our condition, then we also have to believe we are powerless to make a difference and are trapped in our situation with no way out. This is not true! We have the ability to change our lives through Christ! It is the power given by God to every one of His children.

Read the following scriptures and answer the questions.

John 16:33

What are we going to have in this world? ___________________________

Who has overcome the world? ___________________________________

1 John 4:4

Who is the one who is in you? __________________________________

John 15:5

How are we going to prohibit the misfortunes that come our way from becoming the determining factors of our lives?

____

____

____

Bad experiences are a part of life, and we are not always going to be responsible for what comes our way. Sometimes we get to participate in problems that were not of our own making. But we must understand that these things are not what **define** our lives. We cannot control everything that happens to us, but we can **always** control our response to those things. Our responses determine the essence of our lives. As we submit our responses to the authority of God's Word, we will reap a harvest of freedom.

In our own strength, we will never be able to walk out of bad circumstances or conditions. But by abiding in Christ, we can and will walk out of the bondages of our problems and into freedom and victory. If we spend our energy "blaming," we will live in defeat, but if we will accept the responsibility of our response to life, we will be empowered to walk in victory.

I know this lesson may have been extremely difficult for some of you, especially if you have spent much of your life blaming others for your problems. If you are one of those people, I am asking you to not be offended. At the beginning of this study, I told you the journey from where you are to where you want to be in Christ would be the most challenging thing you would ever face. If you won't quit and will continue to embrace the truths of God's Word, you will become everything God intends you to be, and it will be worth all the pain.

As we close our examination of the first area of belief, the "Responsibility of Condition," I want to challenge you to ask the Lord two things. First, ask Him to reveal to you your true condition. He will do this a layer at a time. Secondly, ask Him to work the truth of taking responsibility for yourself in your life. I don't want you to be a victim of circumstance; I want you to be the victor. God will bring this about in the life of anyone willing to embrace His truth. May God grant each of us the grace to face the truth about ourselves, take responsibility for it, and submit it back to Him. Praise His Name!

WEEK THREE

MAIN CONCEPTS

DAY 1: HOW TO AVOID DISCOURAGEMENT ON OUR JOURNEY

DAY 2: DEPENDING ON THE SPIRIT

DAY 3: UNDERSTANDING THE SCOPE OF SATAN'S AUTHORITY

DAY 4: GOD IS IN CONTROL, NOT SATAN

DAY 5: OVERCOMING THE ENEMY

Day One

Condemnation vs. Conviction

If you are still with me after I beat you up so badly last week, then praise the Lord! Let's do a quick review of the principles we have studied together so far. Although we are one being, we are made up of three parts: a body, a soul, and a spirit. After salvation, we are joined with God through the uniting of His Spirit with our spirit. Even though we are one with God in spirit, our minds are in the same conditions after salvation as they were before and are in need of renewal. In other words, we have to learn a new way of thinking.

What we believe dictates the choices we make, which in turn determine the conditions or situations we end up with. How important it is to make sure that our beliefs are in agreement with the Word of God! If what we believe is so important, then Satan has a vested interest in our beliefs and will try diligently to build his strongholds in our minds. A stronghold is an area of our belief system in which we are deceived by Satan and where he has built himself a safe place to carry out his plan for our lives. We talked about the steps we can take to recognize and overcome these strongholds.

In the last few lessons we began our study of the individual areas of our belief systems. The first area of belief we looked at was called the "Responsibility of Condition." It highlighted the importance of recognizing and taking responsibility for ourselves and what we have become. It is not what is brought to each of us that dictates what we become but our responses to those things. If we will embrace the truth of this, we are empowered to help ourselves and stop living the life of a victim.

Today we are going to examine the next area of belief, which I am going to call "Perspective." Perspective represents our belief about *how* we are going to accomplish spiritual advancement.

Every born again believer has a deep seated desire to please God that springs from the Holy Spirit within us. Therefore, as we hear truths such as we must renew our minds, overcome strongholds, take responsibility for ourselves, and the like, we have a sincere desire to change our old ways and walk into the new. We determine to change, and we begin to work really hard to overcome our sins, bad habits, bondage, wrong thinking, and so on. For a while this works, but eventually we fall into a vicious cycle of trying, failing, being discouraged and defeated, without experiencing much lasting victory. This occurs because we have the wrong **perspective** about how to accomplish these goals. Let's look at an example to further explain this point.

Assume that someone we know has done something totally unacceptable and has made us mad; I mean the kind of mad that goes all the way to the bone (I know you know what I'm talking about ☺). Now suppose we have been learning about the need to renew our minds by aligning our thinking with God's Word. We want our decisions to be in agreement with God so that we will reap the fruit of the Spirit, which is life, instead of the fruit of the flesh, which is death. Therefore, we decide to not let our mind dwell on what this person has done. The Word tells us we have to turn the other cheek and forgive them. So, we say to ourselves, "No, I am not going to think about it; I am not going to stay mad; and I am going to forgive them and let it go." That works for about five split seconds, and we have to tell ourselves again. We repeat this at least thirty times in the next half hour. Then our mom or best friend calls, and we just cannot help ourselves; we tell them all about it. When we get off the phone, we are more angry than ever and realize that not only did we fail to not think about it, turn the other cheek, and forgive them; we now get to throw in the sin of gossip on top of not renewing our minds.

This is one of many examples I could give on how we fail so miserably in the process of renewing our minds. After repeatedly failing, we find ourselves feeling condemned. After all, we have finally seen where we are and why we are there, so we can't claim ignorance any more. We know we are supposed to do better; when we don't, not only does our own logical mind condemn us, but Satan is also quick to show us what failures we are. This condition brings about discouragement.

Discouragement is one of the most effective tools of the enemy. Satan knows that if we become discouraged, we lose hope. Hope springs from the belief that we can be different, overcome, grow, and live in victory. Without hope, we stop trying; after all, what's the point if we don't believe we can ever change. This is why Satan continually tries to discourage us.

Many things in our lives can discourage us, but one of the main culprits in the life of a believer is what I mentioned above: condemnation. One of the reasons condemnation is so effective in discouraging us is that it is based on partial truth. As my daddy used to say, "Satan is an expert at dealing in half truths." Condemnation is an emotion that springs from the truth that we have sinned, but the lie that the sin is "on" us. Allow me to clarify something. True condemnation is the condition of being rejected by God. According to scripture, a believer will never experience condemnation. But for the purpose of our discussion, we will define it in the emotional context of how we feel when we have sinned. This type of condemnation brings about the belief that our sin is part of us, that we wear it like a cloak when we enter the presence of God. Often it manifests as a feeling that we need to somehow pay a price for what we have done.

To better understand condemnation, let's contrast it with conviction. Conviction comes when we do something that isn't right, and the Spirit of God within us tells us so. Conviction always comes from God, never from Satan. The purpose of conviction is to enlighten our minds that we might agree with God and repent. At the very moment we say or think, "God, You are right, what I did was wrong. I'm sorry, and I don't want to do that any more. Please help me," conviction has done its job and is gone. The entire purpose of conviction is repentance. Once we agree with God and repent, conviction instantly comes to an end.

Condemnation in the life of a believer, on the other hand, is always from the enemy. Condemnation starts the minute conviction ends. It is Satan's counterfeit for conviction. It feels so similar to conviction that believers often fail to discern the difference. The difference is in the purpose. Where conviction is meant to bring us back into agreement and pure fellowship with God, condemnation is meant to separate us from our Heavenly Father. Conviction is meant to cleanse; condemnation is meant to sully. Condemnation bows down and worships the sin and sinner but gives no homage to the finished work of Christ. Let's compare and contrast these two concepts in scripture.

Read the following passage of scripture and answer the questions.

John 16:7-9

According to this verse, who will convict of guilt? ________________________________

In regard to sin, what are we told is the main conviction? (vs. 9) ______________________

____

The Holy Spirit brings conviction, but the end of conviction is belief in Jesus. When we believe what Jesus tells us and say, "Yes, Lord, you are right, this is sin, I am sorry, please forgive me," conviction ends and our sin is covered by the sacrifice of Jesus. That is what the cross is all about.

Now let's see what the Bible says about the believer and condemnation. Read the following verses and answer the questions.

Mark 16:15-17, John 3:18, John 5:24, 2 Thessalonians 2:12

According to these verses, who will be saved? ___________________________________

Who will be condemned? ____

Condemnation is for the unbeliever, not the believer!

Romans 5:16

What is this verse referring to when it says, "the gift"? ___________________________

What did that gift bring? ____

Read Romans 8:1 and write it on the lines below.

____

____

Believers are never condemned by God. God convicts us and may let us reap the consequences of our actions, but "there is now **NO** condemnation for those who are in Christ Jesus." [emphasis added]

Read Revelation 12:10.

Who is the accuser of the brothers referred to in this verse? ____________________________

If your answer is Satan, you are exactly right. He is the one who accuses us. Satan does not have any authority over a believer; therefore, the only harm he can do to us is if we give him the right by agreeing with him. If we sin, the Holy Spirit convicts us. If we agree with the Spirit and repent (even if we slip up at a future date and do the same sin again), we are cleansed of that sin because of the completed work of Jesus. After this, continued feelings of guilt are the work of the enemy in the form of condemnation. Do not agree with him. Point him to Jesus and the power of the cross.

This concept is extremely difficult for us to accept. We may say we believe it, but in our emotions we really don't. **Jesus Christ was condemned for us.** This is why the accuser was "hurled down." We do not need to allow the enemy's lies to carry more weight with us than God's Word. We must ignore our feelings and rest in the fact that the Word tells us we are no longer condemned. Now, let me clarify that if we are involved in a sin that we don't want to repent of, this is called rebellion and is an entirely different matter. However, if we agree with God and in that moment sincerely repent, God does not condemn us but will forgive us and cleanse us from all unrighteousness (1 John 1:9).

The primary way a child of God can combat the struggle with condemnation and discouragement is to get a new perspective. We want to avoid the trying/failing cycle and move into victorious living. We will discuss how to do this in the next lesson. For now, remember that Jesus took our condemnation when He died on the cross, and He lives to intercede for us. Write Hebrews 7:25 in the space below, and believe it!

Day Two

Perspective

We ended the last lesson with the statement that the primary way for a child of God to combat the struggle with condemnation and discouragement is to get a new perspective. Remember perspective is our belief about *how* we are going to accomplish spiritual advancement. We want to break the cycle of trying and failing and move into victorious living.

Today we will talk about how to do this. The very first thing we must do to break the trying/failing cycle is to realize that there is no way we can ever renew our own minds, deliver ourselves from sin, gain wisdom, etc. It takes God to accomplish these things. If we have the ability, through sheer determination and effort, to actually succeed in overcoming our sin, bondage, wrong thinking, etc., then we don't need Jesus. The Jews tried to do this for generations and were miserable failures.

When we try to obtain spiritual advancement on our own, we are actually exercising self-righteousness, which is offensive to God and results in pride and arrogance. Consider almost everything we do in the flesh. If we work hard enough at anything, whether it's cooking, athletics, music, etc., we will become excellent at it and can justifiably take pride in ourselves. God doesn't allow our spiritual victories to be achieved in this way. He wants us to come to a point where we realize we just can't do it. We have to fall on our face before him and say, "Please do Your work within me, God, because I can't do it!"

Fill in the blanks of **John 15:5**,

> "_______ *am the vine;* __________ *are the branches. If a man* ______________
>
> *in* ___________ *and* _______ *in* ________, *he will bear much fruit;* _________
>
> _________ _________ *you can do* ______________________________."

If we actually believe this verse, we won't waste any more of our time trying to be good. Instead, we will spend our energy figuring out how to remain in Christ. We won't fight our sin as much as we will bring it to the feet of Jesus and say, "I can't, Lord, but you can change my heart. Please do it!" You see, we have wasted so much of our time trying to be good in our own strength that we have missed the opportunity to learn just how good God really is. I spent so much of my life living under feelings of condemnation. I wanted to be good, but I just kept failing. Every time I failed, I felt more condemned. I became so discouraged. I believed the lie of Satan and tried to clean myself up to be good enough to have a relationship with God. Wrong!!! I have learned that the closer I draw to God, the more I tell Him I can't do it on my own, and the more I look to Him and His goodness, the more He cleans me up! He is changing my heart. We are not meant to be slaves to religious behavior. We are meant to learn to know our God and Savior and reflect His glory on others so they can learn to know their God and Savior.

Oh, how my heart is burning with a jealousy for you, my sisters! Satan has done such a number on us. The more we try to be good through our own efforts, the less we will know of God's mercy, goodness, faithfulness, and grace. When I was trying so hard to please God, my Lord's yoke did not feel easy, and His burden did not feel light. They felt like bondage and exhausted me. So, one day I just asked Him, "How can You say that Your yoke is easy and Your burden is light (Matthew 11:30)? It's not! It's not! It's not!" I write this with tears in my eyes. He taught me that I wasn't carrying His yoke or His burden, but was carrying my own and it was bondage. His yoke is easy and His burden is light! He is the one who renews our minds, sets us free, and enables us to take responsibility. We just have to be willing to agree with Him and not give up. We have to keep going and going and going back to Him with our needs. I love the way Martin Luther stated this truth about 500 years ago:

"For if you desire to believe rightly and to possess Christ truly then you must reject all works that you intend to place before and in the way of God. They are only stumbling blocks, leading you away from Christ and from God. Before God no works are acceptable but Christ's own works. Let these plead for you before God, and do no other work before Him than to believe that Christ is doing His works for you and is placing them before God in your behalf. In order to keep your faith pure, do nothing else than stand still, enjoy its blessings, accept Christ's works, and let Him bestow His love upon you." (1)

The beautiful thing about all of this is that when we reach that point of absolute dependency upon Christ, there is very little room for condemnation and discouragement. When we fail, we merely turn to God and say, "Well, I see you're not finished yet." When Satan says, "See what you did," we can say, "You are exactly right. I am stinking rotten. Thank You, God, that I'm not depending on me but on You, the perfecter of my soul. Praise You for what You have done, are doing, and will continue to do in me." As we do this, the enemy's ability to discourage us and cause us to quit is diminished.

The area of belief I call "Perspective" is paramount to our success as Christians. Our perspective about how we are going to renew our minds, overcome our bondage, and take responsibility determines our response to the failures we will most certainly have on our road to victory. When we depend on the finished work of Jesus, we begin to experience victory. Victory causes us to give praise to God and strengthens our faith which leads to more victory. As a result, the trying/failing cycle is broken to be replaced with the trusting/victory cycle.

As we close this lesson, I ask the Father to reveal to us our absolute dependence upon His grace. I pray that we will look to Him, not our own abilities, as we proceed in the sanctification process. Lord Jesus, it's all You!

Day Three

Know Your Enemy

The next area of belief we are going to examine in the light of God's Word is who or what we believe to be our enemy. We each struggle with various things every day that consume our thoughts and energy. I don't know about you, but the older I get, the fewer thoughts and less energy I have to waste. I know you have a desire to progress in the Lord; otherwise, you wouldn't be doing a Bible study. Since we have this great desire to succeed, we certainly don't want to waste time and effort in the process.

As human beings, we are in a continual struggle for survival. As Christians, we have an added challenge of not only survival, but revival. By this I mean that we have to deal with normal things that come into the lives of all people, and must learn to deal with these things according to God's standards. This process of learning to deal with life God's way is what I call personal revival. The greater our personal revival, the more the glory of God will shine forth from our lives, which will cause us to be more attractive to the lost and dying world around us. When they want what we have, we can point them to Jesus. This is what I call peer-revival. As we face our daily struggles, we want to become not only survivors, but also revivers.

Life is a battle, as the old saying goes, and if you don't think so, keep on living. We all know that to win battles we must know our enemy. An army that has no clue who the enemy is cannot fight effectively, and Christians who do not recognize their true enemy will be ineffective warriors as well. If you have been a Christian for any length of time, you are very familiar with the concept that Satan is our enemy. However, there is a huge disparity of beliefs concerning the existence of Satan. The spectrum ranges from those who really do not believe there is a Satan with an army of evil spirits, to the opposite end where we find people who believe every single bad thing that happens is the result of some form of satanic attack. We need to believe rightly about Satan. To do so, we must look to what God has to say about him. Arming ourselves with this knowledge will enable us to be effective in the battles we fight. In week two we read the following verses. Let's revisit them.

1 Peter 5:8	1 Timothy 3:7	2 Timothy 2:26
2 Corinthians 2:11	2 Corinthians 11:14	John 8:44

After reviewing each of these scriptures, we see that Satan is definitely our enemy, and as we discussed in week two, he most certainly has a plan that is diabolically opposed to the plan of God. If you happen to be on the end of the spectrum that doesn't really believe there is a Satan with a host of helpers, then you are going to have to change that belief in order to line up with God's Word. If you want to press on in the Lord, you absolutely cannot say, "Well, I know it says that, but **I think** . . ." God's Word is truth, and we cannot exalt what we think over it and expect to budge one inch in our progress in the Lord.

Now I want to address those at the other end of the spectrum who believe every bad thing that happens is caused by an evil spirit of some sort. This simply isn't true. Take a look at the following scriptures.

James 4:7 | 2 Timothy 4:18 | 1 John 5:18

2 Thessalonians 3:3 | John 17:15

These verses tell us that Jesus will keep us safe, that the evil one cannot harm us. We read that the Lord is faithful and will protect us from the evil one. According to the Bible, the Lord will rescue us from every evil attack; and, if we submit to God, we can resist the devil and he has to flee. Therefore we cannot reduce ourselves to helpless victims in the face of the devil. This is the heritage of the non-believer. We have obviously been given a different heritage, one of power, love, and self discipline (2 Timothy 1:7). If we believe that every bad thing is an attack of the devil, then we also have to believe God isn't living up to His Word. We know this is not the case. So what do we do? What do we believe? On the one hand, we are told we have an enemy; on the other hand, we are told we will be protected from him; and in the middle, we have our life experiences.

Once we become a child of God, the devil has absolutely no power over us unless we give it to him. We are completely under the protection of the blood of Jesus. Read the following verses and answer the questions.

Matthew 28:18

How much authority has been given to Jesus? ______________________________

Luke 10:19

What has Jesus given us? _________________________

How much power of the enemy has Jesus given us the ability to overcome? ____

What will harm us? ____________________________________

If we belong to Christ, we do not have to fear Satan. As stated earlier, he has absolutely no authority over us. We are completely and totally inaccessible to him, at his discretion. After salvation, there are only two ways Satan can have access to us. One is if God allows it in order to fulfill a foreordained purpose. An example of this is the Cross. God allowed Satan admittance to Jesus in order to fulfill God's ultimate plan. The other way that Satan can access us is if we give him permission, then he can have his way. We give him permission in two primary ways, through disobedience and deception.

Disobedience to God opens the door for Satan to come in and produce the fruit of that sin in our lives. For example, if you have sex with someone you are not married to, you could very well get a venereal disease. This would be the work of the enemy seeking to destroy you. However, it would be the result of disobeying the Word that tells you sex outside of marriage is sin, not a satanic attack.

The other way we give Satan access is by believing the lies he tells us. When we do this, he can establish a stronghold in our lives as discussed earlier. An example of this would be if the enemy put thoughts into our minds such as, "My husband is a jerk, he doesn't love me, and frankly I don't love him any more. I think we need a divorce." Agreeing with Satan could bring about the destruction of your family. This would be the fruit of deception.

The two Ds, disobedience and deception, are the only ways we give Satan permission to harm us. In both cases, notice that he has to have our assistance to do it.

If we are fully submitted to God in both thought and deed and are in complete agreement with God's Word, then Satan can do nothing to us or with us, unless God allows it. Obviously these are big "ifs." None of us are fully submitted and in total agreement yet. If we were, we would be perfect. We are vulnerable to the enemy in the areas we are not submitted and are not in agreement with the Word. If this doesn't motivate us to get serious about obedience to God and about exalting His Word, I don't know what will. When we are being attacked by the enemy, our first response should not be to rebuke him but to examine our lives in the areas of obedience and belief. As we submit these areas to God and His Word, we can resist the devil effectively. He will flee!

Day Four

God Is not Our Enemy

In the previous lesson, we established that there is a Satan and that he has a plan which he continually tries to exercise in the life of a believer. We discussed that he has no authority in the life of a Christian and cannot harm us unless either we or God gives him permission. If we are fully submitted to God in both thought and deed and are in complete agreement with God's Word, then Satan can do nothing to us or with us, unless God allows it. He has absolutely no authority over a believer unless we give it to him through disobedience or through believing his lies.

Although these statements are true, there can be some confusion on this issue. Allow me to clarify something in case you are a little confused about the activity of Satan. The fact that Satan has no authority over believers does not mean we won't be affected by anything he does. For example, you might be a fully submitted Christian, but if you are married to an alcoholic, then your life will feel the effects of having a husband that is allowing the enemy to have authority in his life. We are not going to float through life unaffected by any evil activities. Not even Jesus did that.

We will feel the effects of the enemy in this fallen world. However, in the life of a fully submitted believer, Satan will be ineffective in his effort to work his plan. Our lives will accomplish the purposes of God regardless of how hard Satan attacks us. I'm not saying we won't be attacked; I am saying his attacks won't work. Satan even came against Jesus. Think of when the Spirit led Jesus into the desert and Satan came and tempted Him there.

Read Luke 4:1-13.

What does Luke 4:13 say? ____

____

____

Hopefully you answered, "When the devil had finished all this tempting, he left Him until an opportune time." The point I am trying to make is that Jesus was attacked by Satan through temptation, the Pharisees and Sadducees, and any number of other ways the entire time He walked upon this earth. I'm sure Satan thought he had finally conquered the Son of God when he nailed Him to the cross. But all the time that God was allowing Satan to seemingly prevail, the devil was actually working to fulfill God's plan.

Likewise, if we are living our lives in submission to God, then it doesn't matter what Satan tries to do to us. He won't be able to get it done, and whatever he tries will actually fulfill the plan of God in our lives. Ultimately, every single thing that happens to a believer who is living in obedience to God and is walking in the truth of His Word is filtered through the hands of our Father. Nothing gets to us without His allowing it.

If we are a child of God and not living in intentional rebellion, which gives ground to the enemy, everything that happens to us is from His hand, not Satan's. I say this with much compassion in my heart. Things that seem really bad can happen to any of us, even when we are in the dead center of God's will. These things are not from the hand of our enemy; they are from the hand of our God. This may be hard to accept, especially if you are deeply wounded at this time, but hear me on this. Everything that comes to us from the hand of our God is ultimately good. It may not seem that way at the moment, but if we will not turn back and will stay the course, God will bring good from what appears to be bad. I will go so far as to say that the degree of pain suffered will be exceeded by the degree of glory experienced. You may ask, "How could losing my child to cancer ever bring me good?" I cannot answer that for you, but if you will give Him your pain, anger, hurt and bitterness, I know He will give you the answer because His Word says He will. Write Romans 8:28 in the space below and say it out loud as you do so.

God never wastes our pain; there is always a purpose for it. I fully understand that you may be in a place that says, "I don't care what the purpose is; it's not worth it!" But oh, sister, you cannot know that! I have been in that place, and I have seen how wrong I was. Please forgive God so that He can heal your broken heart. If you refuse, you are believing a lie of the enemy and will reap the results of his lordship over your life. Your pain will have been for nothing. God is not your enemy!!!

Please fill in the blanks of one of the most precious verses in the entire Bible, Jeremiah 29:11.

"'I know the ________________ I have for you,' declares the LORD,

'_________ to prosper you and not to ___________ you, ___________

to give you ____________ and a _______________.'"

All things from the hand of God are good. He is working to bring us into His glorious kingdom at the present time and for eternity. I cannot express to you how much freedom I have gained by recognizing that even the bad stuff comes to me from the hand of God, and is for the purpose of forming Jesus Christ within me. I can forgive others so much more easily now because I don't see them as my enemies but rather tools in the hand of God to carve the image of Jesus into my soul. I don't chafe under a difficult circumstance like I used to, because now I recognize it as the sandpaper to smooth my rough edges. I don't fear loss, because I have learned that God gives so much more than He asks. There is much freedom when we stop demanding our rights and rest in His will.

"Oh, Father, heal our broken hearts and teach us to trust You!"

Day Five

Dealing with the Enemy

This week, we have learned that we must have the right perspective about how we are going to accomplish spiritual advancement. We are not going to renew our minds by sheer self-effort, but must look to the Holy Spirit to do within us what we cannot do in ourselves. We learned that we have an enemy who is seeking to work his plan in our lives. He has no authority in the life of a believer unless either God allows him access for a foreordained purpose or we do through disobedience or deception. Lastly, we discussed that God is not our enemy; everything that comes into the life of a submitted believer is from His hand and will be for our benefit. Today we are going to end this week's study with instructions on how to deal with our enemy.

As Christians, one very important responsibility that we have is to pray against the enemy. We do not need to fear him. As we read earlier this week, we have been given all authority over him. We need to exercise that authority. We do this through prayer and the sword of the Spirit, which is the Word of God (Ephesians 6:17).

Satan is aware of his boundaries; this is why he works day and night to get us to sin and exalt our own feelings and thinking above the Word. He tries everything under the sun to get us to give him permission. One major tactic he uses is to get us to believe our true enemy is anything but him. Here is a list of things we might struggle against and perceive to be our enemies:

1. God
2. Spouse
3. Depression
4. Weight
5. Unforgiveness
6. Parents
7. Poverty – lack of resources
8. Siblings
9. Friends or co-workers
10. Self-image
11. Those who do us wrong
12. Lack of faith
13. Our culture
14. Our sin

This list could go on forever. The point is that Satan doesn't mind us struggling against any of these things. He's happy when we struggle against them, and spends a lot of time trying to get us to believe these things are our problems. If he can get us to focus on the circumstance, we are not going to be any danger to him. He doesn't even mind when we fight so hard against our sin.

Even though he cannot appropriate the principles of God, Satan understands them probably better than we do. He spent time in heaven with God before he decided he wanted to be God and was subsequently kicked out. He also has had thousands of years to observe human nature and the interaction between God and man. Satan totally understands the effects of renewing our minds, and knows that if we begin to line our thinking up with God's Word, he is fighting a losing battle. He knows he has no access to us without our permission. This is why he does everything he can to get us to agree with him through disobedience and deception. We do not need to fear Satan; we need to fear missing God, which is the only way we can be truly harmed.

None of the previously mentioned things are our enemies; they merely represent the circumstances in our lives. As we learned in week two, it's not what is brought to us that dictates our lives but what we do with what is brought. Things and people are not our enemies. Satan and his forces are whom we battle.

Look at Ephesians 6:11-13.

According to these verses, what "things" are **not** our true enemies?

List the things this scripture tells us **are** our true enemies. (hint: There are 2 primary enemies).

1. _________________, _______________, and _______________ of this

dark world, and

2. ____________ ________________ _____ ________ in the heavenly realms (NIV)

According to this passage, we do not struggle against flesh and blood but against rulers, against authorities, against the powers of this dark world, and against the spiritual forces of evil in the heavenly realms.

If we will allow the Holy Spirit to open our minds to understand that our true struggle is not in our circumstances but with an enemy set to deceive and destroy us, then we will stop wasting time and energy on fighting one another or our circumstances and begin to do true harm to the real foe. Stop fighting with your husband; he's not your real enemy. Quit trying to stop sinning so hard; sin isn't the root problem. Stop being mad at God; He's your only hope.
I pray that our hearts will begin to realize that our struggle really isn't with flesh and blood but with the spiritual forces of evil that work so hard to deceive us.

Having established that our true enemy is Satan, let's close this lesson by discussing how to deal with him. Read the following scriptures and record what specific instructions we are given in each one regarding how we are to handle our enemy.

Ephesians 4:27

____

1 Peter 5:9

____

James 4:7

____

In these verses, we see the following instructions:

1. Do not give the devil a foothold. How do we give the devil a foothold? Through disobedience and deception - believing Satan's lies.

2. Resist him, stand firm in the faith. How do we do this? By exalting what God says above everything: thought, feeling, sight, and experience. For example, we might say something to this effect, "Satan, I know you are making me feel X, but God says in His Word Y. I am going to believe what He says over what you are saying."

3. Submit ourselves to God. We do this by believing what He says and obeying Him, by not giving up even when it hurts, and by bowing to His will even when it's the hardest thing we have ever done.

One final point: never underestimate the power of prayer and praise. When we are in a situation in which we sense the presence of our enemy, we need to pray and ask God to show us how to resist in that given moment. He is faithful and will show us. Lastly, do not forget to praise and thank God for His goodness and His promises; this drives the enemy crazy. When God is being exalted in any way, the devil will not hang around.

As we refuse to give the devil access into our lives and as we submit to God and resist the enemy, we will walk in more and more freedom. Satan will not be able to work his plan in our lives. I pray the eyes of our hearts will be opened to see our true enemy and that we will begin to fight him with the weapons we have been given. Prayerfully read this final verse and ask the Lord to teach you to be a mighty warrior in His army.

> *"For though we live in the world, we do not wage war as the world does. The weapons we fight with are not the weapons of the world. On the contrary, they have divine power to demolish strongholds. We demolish arguments and every pretension that sets itself up against the knowledge of God, and we take captive every thought to make it obedient to Christ."*
>
> *2 Corinthians 10:3-5*

WEEK FOUR

MAIN CONCEPTS

DAY 1: THE WAY INFORMATION ENTERS OUR MINDS

DAY 2: THE IMPORTANCE OF WHAT WE PUT INTO OUR MINDS

DAY 3: DETERMINING HOW TO SPEND OUR TIME

DAY 4: UNDERSTANDING THE TRUTH ABOUT TRUTH

DAY 5: UNDERSTANDING THAT ALL TRUTH COMES FROM GOD

Day One

Channels of Input

Last week we discussed the importance of knowing our true enemy. One of the points we discussed was that the only way the enemy can access the life of a believer is through disobedience or deception. We are going to begin this week by delving a little deeper into how to keep ourselves from being deceived and how to become more obedient. If Satan's only access into our lives is through our cooperation by disobeying God or believing his lies, then we want to learn how to stop doing these things.

We established very early in this study that our minds are the control centers of our lives. Our minds receive input from our bodies and our spirits, then analyze the data received and make choices. Our minds then give instructions to our bodies, and our bodies carry forth the instructions the best that they can. Sometimes my mind tells my body to do things it can't, such as, "Do one-hundred sit ups in three minutes." In this case, my mind has been given false information. ☺ Ha! Ha! In all seriousness, this little jest holds a truth we need to examine. The information we put into our minds will affect the choices our minds make. This is the next area of our belief system we are going to examine – our belief about the importance of what we put into our minds.

Many Christians have never really considered the importance of what they allow their minds to dwell on. Therefore they do not jealously guard what they put into their minds. I am going to call the mind in this condition a passive mind. Before the Holy Spirit opened my understanding to this principle, I never really considered taking note of what I let fill my mind as I went about my day. When I began to think about this, I realized that much of my days were spent with a very passive mind. I just thought about whatever popped into my head, and it never occurred to me that I had much control over it. Considering the fact that our minds analyze everything and make our choices, it stands to reason we would want to stand guard over the doorway of our minds.

Write Proverbs 4:23 in the space below.

According to Strong's Hebrew Definitions, the word heart in this particular verse comes from the word "labe" and means "inner man, mind, will, heart, understanding." Therefore this verse is telling us that above all else we are to guard our minds. When the Word says something like "above all else," it behooves us to listen to what it says. How many of us are seriously guarding the things we allow to enter our minds and the minds of our children? Our beliefs about this have a massive effect upon our lives, even if we are unaware of it.

To reiterate: What we allow our minds to dwell on will have a major impact on the decisions we make. Our five senses and our spirits are the channels through which information enters our minds. Let's take a look at each of these channels and see the types of things from which each of these are receiving input.

1. **The sense of hearing:** what things we hear or listen to

   Examples are:

   CDs, ipods, radio, telephone, conversation, what we let come out of our mouths, sounds of stillness and quiet, etc.

2. **The sense of sight:** what we look at or watch

   Examples are:

   television, the computer, books, magazines, pictures, etc.

3. **The sense of smell:** what we encounter in the air around us.

   Examples are:

   clean fresh air, cigarette smoke infested air, chemicals of other kinds, drugs, etc.

4. **The sense of touch:** what our skin comes into contact with

   Examples are:

   human contact such as a hug, pat, or a sock in the nose ☺; contact such as our hand feeling something rough or smooth; the feeling of cold, cool, warm, or hot, etc.

5. **The sense of taste:** what goes into our mouths

   Examples are:

   food, drink, medicine, drugs, etc.

6. **Our spirit** - the channel from which we hear the Holy Spirit

When we think of the senses as channels of input into our minds, a few of them seem a little humorous. But really, if you think about it, the principle applies to each one of them. If we are talking about living a victorious Christian life, then each of these channels has an impact. Let's think of the least likely sense to affect our lives, the sense of smell. What we smell sends a message to our minds. If I walk into my house and smell homemade bread, the message sent to my mind is "come on in!" If I walk in and smell smoke, the message to my mind is "something is wrong." Both of these messages affect my next decision. The same is true with every sense we have.

Understanding the input channels into our minds will enable us to become more alert to what is flowing through those channels. Tomorrow we will continue this discussion. For now let's ask the Lord to help us become more aware of the information we allow into our minds. See you next time!

Day Two

Data In

In the last lesson, we talked about the channels of input into our minds. Our fives senses and our spirits are the avenues for information into our minds. Considering the fact that our minds are the control centers of our lives, it only makes sense to realize the importance of what we put into our minds.

If we want to outsmart our enemy and learn to think properly, we must guard each of these channels carefully. What are we watching? What are we reading? What are we listening to? I have heard over and over again in my life, "I don't listen to the words of songs; I just listen to the music." If you allow this belief to reign, you are allowing the enemy access into your mind in this area. I want to share with you a personal story that relates to this particular example. My first husband left me a note on the table one day telling me he did not love me any more and wanted a divorce. At that time, there was a very popular country song out, and one of the lines in the song said, "I wouldn't be this lonely all by myself." In the note, my ex-husband wrote this exact line. Without even realizing it, he was copying a song he had been listening to. I had been available to him any time he needed or wanted me. I hadn't been closing him out on any level. I'm not saying that listening to this song was the sole reason he decided to end our marriage. I am saying the words of this song had entered his mind and were having an effect.

Everything we allow into our minds has an effect. If we are watching, listening to, or talking a bunch of junk, it is affecting our minds. Now, before you ease your conscience with "Oh, I don't watch junk," let's define junk. Read Philippians 4:8 and record everything this verse tells us we are to think about.

____

____

____

This is a pretty high standard isn't it? When God began to deal with Bruce (my wonderful husband) and me about this issue, we had been discussing with our boys why they were not allowed to see some of the things their friends were watching. We whipped out good old Philippians 4:8 and read it to them. Well, being the precious, tenderhearted children that they are, they said, "You're right Mom and Dad; we don't want to watch that stuff." They were the ages of three, seven, and nine at the time. ☺ That very night, Bruce and I watched one of the Bourne Identity movies. We loved it, but it was way too violent for our kids. Therefore, we let them watch another movie in the other room. The next morning our oldest son, David, came in and saw the case for our movie and asked me in complete innocence, "Mom, does this movie line up with the verse you read to us yesterday?" Let me tell you, I was cut to the heart. When Bruce got home that night I told him, "I refuse to tell my kids to live by a standard I'm not living by myself." He completely agreed. That very night, we wrote Philippians 4:8 on a piece of paper and took every DVD we owned and compared it with that scripture. Needless to say, we got rid of most of our favorite movies. Please hear me when I say that I do not think everyone has to do this. This was how the Spirit led us. I'm also not saying anything against Matt Damon; he is an obvious hunk ☺! But if we want to live the powerful, effective life we see in scripture and in the lives of certain saints throughout the ages, we have to get serious about lining our lives up with the Word.

We not only have to guard what we put in our minds, but we also have to diligently guard what we allow our minds to think about. When we just think about whatever pops into our heads and don't hold our thoughts to the standard of God's Word, we are operating with passive minds. A passive mind is the devil's playground. Unless we are actively putting good stuff into our minds and actively controlling what we are thinking, we will automatically put in and think on the wrong things. As I stated earlier, when God began to reveal this truth to me, I realized that many of my days were spent with a very passive mind. It had never occurred to me that I could control my thoughts. I have literally allowed an incident to control my thoughts for days. I call this obsessive thinking. Obsessive thinking is not of God. Some examples of thoughts that can become obsessive are:

1. What someone said or did that upset us.
2. Worry about

    a. our kids
    b. our husbands
    c. our looks
    d. our health
    e. our future
    f. our finances
    g. what someone thinks of us
    h. what we did that was stupid

3. How someone can be the way he or she is

The list could go on forever. When obsessive thoughts are coupled with our feelings and emotions, they can absolutely control our entire day or longer. There have been days during which I treated my husband and kids terribly, because I was allowing something to control my thoughts. I should have turned the issue over to God and then let go. To turn something over to God and then let it go sounds simple enough, but it is so hard to actually accomplish.

I can tell you from experience that there is no way we can control our thinking by sheer force of will. It is impossible. The only way to gain victory in this area is to actively pursue putting good things into our minds and allowing the Spirit to supernaturally rejuvenate our thinking.

In the same way that what we eat and how much we exercise determines how healthy our bodies are going to be, what we put in our minds and how we act on that determines how healthy our minds are going to be. If we drink soda and eat chips and candy bars all the time instead of eating healthful foods, we are not going to have healthy bodies. If we don't eat or drink anything at all, we are still going to be unhealthy. In the same way, if we let our minds feast on junk or if we just let our minds do whatever, we are not going to have healthy minds. We have to make a conscious choice to put good things into our minds. As we fill our minds with the things of God, through the power of the Holy Spirit, right thinking will begin to prevail. This is how we become more obedient and less deceived, which, if you will recall, closes Satan's access into our lives.

What are some of the good things we can put into our minds? Remember good is defined in Philippians 4:8.

1. God's Word
2. Scriptural, Godly teaching
3. Inspirational music
4. Positive confession
5. Edifying conversation
6. Noble thoughts

It is important to note that we can put in good stuff, but if we don't act on it, it will do us no good. We can fill our mouths with good, healthful food, but unless we chew it up and swallow, it will do nothing to bring health to our bodies. There are a lot of people who read their Bibles, listen to Christian music and teaching, and claim to be seeking God, but there is no evidence of the fruit of the Spirit in their lives. Unless we act on what we are putting in, we will receive very little benefit.

Read James 1:22-25.

What do these verses warn us not to do? ______________________________

____

With what does this passage compare one who listens to the Word but does not do what it says?

____

____

What does this scripture say will happen to the man who continues to look into and do what the

Word says? ______________________________

____

We need to believe rightly about the importance of what we are putting in and keeping out of our minds. Our lives will bear the fruit of what we feed our minds. I want to challenge each of us to let 2 Corinthians 10:5 be our instruction manual for how we deal with every thought that enters our minds. Please write it in the space below and ask the Lord to make this a reality in your life.

Praise the Lord! He will do even more than we ask!

Day Three

Setting Priorities

The next area I want to broach is our belief about the importance of setting priorities. In our culture we have been made to believe that a busy life equals a full life. Without consciously doing so, we have bought into the idea that busy means successful. Considering the fact that I am home-schooling three boys; teaching a women's Sunday School class; writing this study; and trying to keep my house clean and the laundry caught up, exercise consistently, cook three meals a day, and be a good wife, mother, friend, daughter, etc., this is an area very near to my own heart.

There are twenty-four hours in every day, and we are going to be doing something in every one of them. What we do each hour adds up to what we do each day, each week, each year, and ultimately what we do with our lives. Time is the one thing we cannot stop, and, once spent, can never be regained; it's gone forever. It's the one commodity that no one can cheat and as long as we are alive, we all have the exact same amount of it every day.

My hope in this lesson is to stir the desire to stop and think about what we are buying with the time we are spending. Then we can make the necessary adjustments in our lives to bring them into the balance that God intends for His people.

I'm not promoting the "don't worry, be happy" mentality. There is nothing spiritual about laziness and passivity. God wants His people to be fruitful. However, He wants to direct the how, why, when, where, and what we do. Take a look at the following verses and answer the questions.

Ephesians 2:10

What were we created in Christ Jesus to do? ______________________________

Who prepared them in advance for us? ______________________________

Thought: God has a detailed plan for our lives. From the moment we are conceived, He not only personally forms who we are and the way we are put together, (gives us our personalities and our physical attributes), He also has a specific plan for each of our lives. Read the following scriptures and answer the questions.

Psalm 139:13

Who created your inmost being? ____________________________

Who knit you together in your mother's womb? ________________

Psalm 139:15-17

Is God aware of your frame (body)? ________

When were all the days ordained for you written in God's book? _____________

____

Jeremiah 1:4-5

Who formed Jeremiah in the womb? ______________

When did God **know** him? ____

When was Jeremiah set apart? ____

When did God appoint him as a prophet to the nations? ____________________

____

At that point, had Jeremiah done anything good or bad to make him worthy or not worthy for such a calling? _________________

Before our God formed us, He knew us and set us apart. He has a most definite plan for every one of us; we need to believe this if we are ever going to be willing to prioritize our lives to fulfill His plan. As long as we live under the erroneous belief that God just isn't that interested in the details, we won't be very serious about finding out what He wants in those details. Little details added together are what form the greater picture of our lives.

Satan understands God has a plan, and it is his greatest ambition to thwart it. He works overtime to cloud our thinking in this area. One way he does this is by deceiving us into becoming so busy that we don't have time to think. We run around living life and are so busy and stressed that we have no time to ponder and often fail to hear God's voice. We do not recognize the hand of Satan in this; it just seems like life. But he is most definitely behind this type of busyness. Remember, he also has a detailed plan for our lives.

If we do not make a conscious decision to set our priorities in accordance with God's plan for us, we will automatically set the priorities that will fulfill Satan's plan. This may seem like a severe statement, but it is nonetheless true. If we were on the same level with God or Satan, then we might possibly be able to fulfill our own plan, but we are by far inferior beings to both God and Satan. Satan is not smarter, stronger, or more powerful than God, but he most certainly is more of everything than we are, in and of ourselves. Therefore we will follow one or the other. So, I say again, if we are not diligently seeking to know and set God's priorities for our lives, we will automatically align ourselves with the priorities of the devil. The devil's priorities do not always look evil; however, they are always an alternative to God's.

Having established this, how do we know the priorities of God for our lives? If you are anything like me, you have spent X number of years way more interested in your own priorities than God's. When that doesn't work, you begin to have a change of heart and decide that maybe you should pay more attention to God's way of doing things. You then have a changed heart but do not know what God wants you to do; you haven't exactly learned to hear His voice all that well. If this is where you find yourself, what should you do?

I wish I could give you the "Ten Steps to Prioritizing Your Life in Accordance With God's Will." But it's not that simple. Only God knows the detailed plan He has for each one of us. We have to get it straight from Him. I can't tell you how to prioritize your life, but what I **can** do is give you a place to start. Fill in the blanks of Psalm 116:1.

> *"I love the Lord, for he _______________ _______ ___________; he heard my ________ for mercy."*

First, we bow before Him, acknowledge our willfulness, and cry out to Him for His mercy. Our prayer might be something like this: "Father, I have chosen my own way for a long time now. I have decided the way I should go, and I don't like where it has taken me. Please forgive me. Lord, I want to change and do things Your way, but I don't have any idea exactly what that is. Please lead me step by step into Your way of doing things. Show me what You want me to do and the way you want me to do it. Show me what's important and what isn't. Help me to learn to hear Your voice giving me direction in the details. Thank You for hearing my cry, in Christ's name. Amen!"

Now, turn to Psalm 119:9-10 and fill in the blanks.

> *"How can a young man keep his way pure? By living ____________________ _____ ___________ ____________. I seek you with _________ my heart; do not let me stray from your commands."*

After we repent of our willfulness and cry out to God, we must learn how God feels about things. We do this through reading His Word. We have been given a tremendous gift in the Bible, for it is a letter straight from the heart of God to us. He gave it to us that we might know Him. Every time we read the Bible, we are learning how He feels, what He thinks, what He wants from us, what we can expect from Him, and many other things. It's not just a book of rules, as people often believe. It is the revelation of who God is. As we become familiar with what the Bible has to say, we begin to grow in our understanding of God. This enables us to become more attuned to His voice so that when He speaks to us, we recognize it.

It is very much like learning a foreign language. If you have ever tried to learn a foreign language, you know that when you first start it is like listening to a bunch of gibberish; you cannot understand anything. But as you familiarize yourself with individual words, you slowly begin to distinguish them when listening to conversation. After a while, you actually understand sentences and eventually can fully communicate with a person speaking in the language. With God it is very similar. You begin by acquainting yourself with the Word. Little by little, you become aware of how God thinks, and begin to recognize His opinions about things. Finally you are intimately communicating with God, ascertaining what He wants you to do. This is how we learn to set the priorities of God in our lives.

Psalms 119:11 says, “I have hidden your word in my heart that I might not sin against you.” If we are serious about fulfilling God’s plan for our lives, we will hide His Word in our hearts.

In closing, let me say once again: I cannot give you the detailed plan of God’s priorities for your life. I can tell you that the first two should be to cry out to God and get into His Word. He will take you from there. If you will seriously seek Him with all your heart, He truly will lead you step by step into His perfect will. He is so faithful. Let’s close by writing Matthew 6:33 on the lines below.

____

____

____

____

Day Four

There Is Truth

For the remainder of this week we are going to examine our beliefs about truth, what truth is, and the importance of where we go to establish our basis of truth. We all live lives based on certain things we believe to be true. This relates back to the principle we talked about in week one that what we believe determines the choices we make, which determine the outcome of our lives. Truth is important!

There is an underlying attitude in our culture today that there are no absolutes, truth is subjective, and everything is relative to its situation. It is the ideology that nothing is unwaveringly true. If one dares to say there are absolutes, he or she is dubbed close-minded, harsh, unloving, judgmental, naïve, and any number of other negative labels. We need to believe rightly about this issue.

Let's begin with the basic definition of truth. According to the Random House Dictionary, truth is defined as:

> "The true or actual state of a matter; conformity with fact or reality, verity; a verified or indisputable fact, proposition, principle, or the like; actuality or actual existence."

I particularly like the terms "fact," "reality," and "actual" used in this definition. I am unapologetically going to make the following statement:

There is an absolute truth about every single thing in our lives.

Regardless of what we are dealing with, there is a fact, reality, and actuality in it. We may not know what that is, but it exists nonetheless. In every instance, there are usually three perspectives. 1.) What we believe to be true, 2.) What we want to be true, and 3.) What is true. In the perfect situation, all three perspectives agree.

Let's look at a few examples to clarify this point.

Example 1: Currently, my husband and I are trying to decide if we should buy a house that we can rent for additional income. The question is: Will this be a sound financial decision for our family? In this situation, the first two perspectives are in agreement. We believe it would benefit us financially to buy the house, and we most certainly want the purchase to benefit us financially. The problem comes with the third perspective. In reality, will it actually benefit us financially?

Example 2: I enjoy drinking Diet Dr Pepper, which is sweetened with aspartame. I have read and heard information saying aspartame is very dangerous and can cause problems with one's health. Diet Dr Pepper is sweetened with aspartame. The question is: Will drinking Diet Dr Pepper actually hurt me? In this situation, the three perspectives do not necessarily agree. I personally believe it probably isn't good for me. I want drinking Diet Dr Pepper to be perfectly safe. I have no idea what the actual truth about this is.

Example 3: I have to go to town every Thursday in order for my children to participate in what we homeschoolers call co-op classes. Therefore, it is my desire to get all of my "town" obligations packed into this one day. If I do this, I can be home the rest of the week. In order to accomplish this goal, I have to do all of the following things on Thursday:

- Grocery shopping
- David and Matt's piano lesson
- Luke's drum lesson
- 4 hours of co-op classes
- David and Matt's football practice/game
- three meals out (expensive with five people)
- usually a trip to either Lowe's, Hobby Lobby, Staples, or Wal-mart for some sort of supplies
- any appointment for hair, nails, medical, or business
- errands for Bruce or the kids

The question is: Can this be accomplished? In this situation, the first and the last perspectives happen to agree; the second doesn't. I don't really believe I can fit all of these activities into one day. I want this to be possible, but the fact is, it is not possible. There are only 24 hours in a day, and in our town, most of the businesses are only open from 8:00 a.m. to 5:00 p.m. It isn't physically possible to fit it all in.

In each of these examples, there is an actual truth. Knowing this truth will enable me to make decisions that will bring me good instead of harm. Knowing the truth about the financial soundness of buying a rent house will allow me to make a decision that will bring about the desired result – financial increase. Knowing the truth about aspartame will allow me to make a decision that will bring about the desired result – either enjoying the soda worry free or avoiding harm to my health. Knowing the truth about what I can actually accomplish on Thursday will allow me to make a choice that will bring about the desired result – not stressing myself and my family out every Thursday.

These are just a few simple examples from my own life that show the importance of knowing truth. There are much greater issues of truth at stake. Did God create the world in six literal days or is evolution true? Is Jesus Christ the only way to heaven or are there many paths? Is the Bible the infallible Word of God or just a book of wisdom? Is there really a God? We see many conflicting ideas all around us. I am proposing that there is an absolute truth about each of them. If we want to make wise choices in our lives, we need to know that truth.

Most of us tend to try to make truth fit into what we want. Truth is truth, and is unchanging. Our opinion about a truth has no effect upon that truth. Our opinion only affects what happens to us in each situation. For example, suppose the actual truth about aspartame is that it can cause brain tumors. Just because I believe it is harmless and continue to consume large amounts of it doesn't change the fact that it can cause brain tumors. My opinion only affects my chance of getting one. We need to understand that truth will not conform to our opinions. Truth will stand.

In refusing to seek the truth about things, we bring much harm to ourselves. We must learn to see the value of absolute truth. We may think we want something to be a certain way and make our decisions accordingly, but in the end we will pay a price. Truth is protection, even when it is painful to embrace. The ideology that there are no absolutes will bear the fruit of chaos in the life of the person who lives accordingly. If you don't believe me, take a look at our society.

I want to stimulate our hearts to desire truth, for truth is our friend; and only in knowing it are we empowered to make accurate decisions about the things we face. We are all tempted to filter truth through the screen of our own ideology, and often feel threatened by anything challenging what we believe or desire. This is the wrong attitude. In whatever we face, we should seek to know the truth, not discredit it. Let's close this lesson by asking the Father to enable us to embrace truth!

Day Five

What Is Truth?

After yesterday's lesson, I hope we are beginning to see the necessity of truth. Today, let's switch gears and talk about where we go to establish truth. How do we know what truth really is, and where do we find it?

In answering these questions, I want to begin by saying that for believers in Christ one of the first truths that must be established is the credibility of God's Word. Is the Bible the infallible, inspired Word of God? Until this issue is settled, there is no reason to go any further, because the foundation of all true Christian doctrine is that very same Word.

Allow me to raise a few questions. If we do not believe the Bible is God's unerring, holy Word from beginning to end, why believe any of it? If one part of it isn't true, how do we know the part about grace and salvation is true? If some of it can't be trusted, none of it can. If we place our faith in the part about salvation, we should also place our faith in the rest of it. Why would we place our faith in a God who can't be trusted to give an accurate account of Himself and His dealings with man? Is it beyond the scope of God's ability to anoint prophets to record His heart in a book that is infallible? If so, why trust Him on any level? If this is beyond His ability, why in the world would we trust Him to keep us out of hell? To believe in God but not His Word is irrational, considering the fact that what we know of God is primarily derived from the Bible. If the Bible is not to be trusted, we are left with the untenable condition of man defining God instead of God defining Himself. If we choose to believe in God, then is it such a stretch to also believe He is able to record in writing a description of Himself, His likes and dislikes, His requirements for relationship, and a history of His dealings with man?

We cannot prove that God does or does not exist; belief in Him is based on faith alone. We cannot prove or disprove His Word, either. Here also belief requires pure faith. Regardless of what we choose to believe, it will be based on faith, either in God and His Word or in our own intellect. To believe in God and not His Word renders God subject to our intellect and thus once again demands a faith in ourselves.

If you are a Christian, God's Word must become the measuring rod of all truth. John 17:17 tells us that God's Word is truth. Again in Romans 3:4 Paul makes the statement, "Let God be true, and every man a liar." You are going to have to decide where to place your faith. As for me, I believe every word in the Bible is the inspired, infallible Word of God. I am basing my entire life on it. God and His Word are my life, and I am trusting in Him to make everything work according to His will.

To be a Christian and not believe in the Bible is to build your house on "the sand" (Matthew 7:26). You will be as James 1:6 says, ". . . he who doubts is like a wave of the sea, blown and tossed by the wind. That man should not think he will receive anything from the Lord; he is a double-minded man, unstable in all he does." It is important to believe rightly about the Word of God.

When we place our faith in God and His Word, many questions are answered. Jesus is the only way to heaven. Why? Because the Bible tells us in John 14:6. God did create the World in six literal days. Why? Because the first chapter of Genesis tells us so. When we choose to place our faith in the Word, it becomes our measurement of truth. This entire study is based on this principle.

God is the God of all truth! Fill in the blanks of the following verses.

Psalm 31:5

"Into your hands I commit my spirit; redeem me, O LORD, the ______ ______ _________."

Isaiah 65:16

"Whoever invokes a blessing in the land will do so by the ______ ____ ________; he who takes an oath in the land will swear by the ______ ____ _______. For the past troubles will be forgotten and hidden from my eyes."

These two verses were written under the leadership of the Holy Spirit by two different men, centuries apart. They use the same wording. They do not say that God is the God of "A truth or "the truth." They say He is the God of truth. These passages are telling us that there is no truth outside of God. God is the God of all truth, and the reality of this is available to us through His Son. Read the following verses and answer the questions.

John 1:14

Jesus came full of what? ____

John 1:17

Truth came through whom? ______________________________________

John 14:6

In this scripture, Jesus said He is three things. What are they? ______________

____

Jesus lived, died, and rose again to provide a way for us to live in total fellowship with God. Remember God is three in one – Father, Son, and Holy Spirit. His desire is that we be one with Him, and He desires for us to participate in all that He is. This can be clearly seen in John 17:20-21,

> *"My prayer is not for them alone. I pray also for those who will believe in me through their message, 21 that all of them may be one, Father, just as you are in me and I am in you. May they also be in us so that the world may believe that you have sent me."*

We are able to participate in Christ through the Spirit that He gave us. Read the following passages of scripture. [emphasis added]

John 14:16-20

> *"And I will ask the Father, and he will give you another Counselor to be with you forever— 17* ***the Spirit of truth****. The world cannot accept him, because it neither sees him nor knows him. But you know him, for* ***he lives with you and will be in you****. 18 I will not leave you as orphans; I will come to you. 19 Before long, the world will not see me anymore, but you will see me. Because I live, you also will live. 20 On that day you will realize that I am in my Father, and you are in me, and I am in you."*

John 14:25-27

> *"All this I have spoken while still with you. 26 But the Counselor, the Holy Spirit, whom the Father will send in my name, will teach you* ***all things*** *and will remind you of everything I have said to you. 27 Peace I leave with you; my peace I give you. I do not give to you as the world gives. Do not let your hearts be troubled and do not be afraid.*

The Holy Spirit is the Spirit of truth because He is God's Spirit. It is through the Holy Spirit we have access to all truth. Christ made this possible through His sacrifice. In week one, we discussed that when we put our faith in this sacrifice our spirit becomes one with God's; this is known as salvation. It is through salvation that we have the capacity to partake of all that Jesus died to give us. Part of what He died to give us is the ability to know truth. If you are like me, you tend to associate the truth of God with spiritual truth. That is definitely the truth that undergirds all truth, but I want us to recognize all truth encompasses all things. Therefore, the Spirit is here to guide us into all truth about all things. The Spirit most assuredly wants us to understand the deep truths of God. However, He also wants to guide us in practical things as well, things such as whether or not to buy a rent house, whether or not to consume aspartame, and whether or not to schedule everything on one day.

The Holy Spirit not only reveals truth to us, He also enables us to appropriate that truth into our lives. Often the Spirit will bring us truth, but we don't really want to hear it. Therefore we refuse to receive that truth. When this happens, the Spirit will convict our conscience regarding the issue until we come into agreement with Him. Then as we confess our hesitancy to agree with Him, He will change our hearts on the matter. Let's use the aspartame issue as an example. Assume the Spirit has tried to inform me of the dangers of drinking too much Diet Dr Pepper. But I like it so much that I am unwilling to stop drinking it. The Spirit will not force me to stop drinking the soda, but He will convict me about it until I finally say, "Okay, you are right. I need to quit." I might then confess to Him that I am not able to stop drinking it on my own and ask Him to help me have the willpower to stop. He is faithful and will help me. This would be an example of the Holy Spirit enabling us to appropriate truth.

You may ask, "Do you really believe the God whom created the entire universe will impart truth to you about whether or not to consume aspartame?" My answer is an adamant YES! He has been faithful to me in this way over and over again. If we will take the time to seek Him about every single thing we deal with, then He will impart truth to us regarding it. He is so faithful! The problem is that so many times we don't believe He cares about the little details of our lives, and we fail to seek the truth from Him.

Because of this, we receive information about our various things from sources other than Him. When we get our information apart from Him, we risk believing something to be true when in fact it is not. God can bring us truth through any avenue He so chooses. He doesn't always impart truth to us in a supernatural way, e.g. visions, prophecy, etc. He may cause us to come into contact with someone who has done first hand study of aspartame and its effect on the body. He can impart truth to us however He wants. The point is, we can be very secure in the truth He reveals. We can know it is the real truth, because it came from Him.

The answer to the question "How do we know what truth really is?" is found by answering the question "Where do we find it?" As we look to God to meet all our needs, we can know the truth about whatever we face. If He is our source of information, then we can know the information He brings to us is truth.

It is extremely important that we believe rightly about truth. If we do not believe there is absolute truth, we will not seek to find it. If we do not seek to find all truth in God, we risk finding answers that are not really true. If we find the wrong answers, we will make wrong choices. If we make wrong choices, we suffer. I want to challenge you to begin looking to God for His truth in every situation you face – big or small. Let's close this lesson by writing Psalm 25:5 in the space below.

How I pray this becomes the prayer of our hearts.

WEEK FIVE

MAIN CONCEPTS

DAY 1: FAITH IS THE FOUNDATION OF THE CHRISTIAN EXPERIENCE

DAY 2: THE NEED TO EXERCISE OUR FAITH

DAY 3: BEING FAITHFUL WITH WHAT WE HAVE BEEN GIVEN

DAY 4: DOUBT AND UNBELIEF ARE ENEMIES OF OUR FAITH

DAY 5: HOW TO COMBAT THESE ENEMIES

Day One

The Importance of Faith

Let's begin this lesson with a quick review of what we have discussed over the last couple of weeks. In week three we examined the belief I called perspective. It is very important to have the right understanding of how to accomplish spiritual advancement. By realizing our absolute dependency on Christ to work His nature within us, we can avoid the pitfalls of condemnation and discouragement.

Next, we talked about the need to recognize our true enemy. Our struggle is not with the people and situations in our lives; it is with the rulers, authorities, and powers of this dark world and with the spiritual forces of evil in the heavenly realms (Ephesians 6:11-12). We do not have to be afraid of the devil. Our greatest weapon against him is to be in the center of God's will.

Then, we examined the belief about the importance of guarding the data we allow into our minds. We must be watchful about what we allow our minds to think on. Just as what we eat has an effect on our physical health, what we allow our minds to feed on will have an effect on our spiritual wellbeing.

We began week four talking about the importance of setting God's priorities in our lives. This can be done by learning to know God and learning to hear His voice. We closed the week by discussing the importance of truth. God is the God of truth, and He must be our source of truth. If we get our information from God, we can know that the information we receive is, in fact, truth.

We will begin this week by examining our belief about faith. At first glance, one might wonder at the importance of scrutinizing belief about faith. Faith is faith, isn't it? Considering the fact that faith is the backbone of our relationship with God, I believe it is important to think rightly about it. This is an area in our belief system in which many people do not understand truth, or, in other words, are in error. As we discussed in the last lesson, knowing truth is important. In order for us to properly grow in the Lord, we need to understand the truth about faith.

Let's begin by looking at several scriptures to establish the importance of faith. After this, we will examine what faith is and how we strengthen it. Before we start looking at these passages, I want to clarify that "to believe" and "to have faith" are one and the same. Some of the following verses are going to use the word faith, and some are going to use the term believe or believed. Understand that the message is the same. To believe is to have faith, and to have faith is to believe.

On the following page is your homework for this lesson. Although it is extensive, it really is worth the effort. Turn to that page now and follow the instructions.

Hopefully this exercise has enlightened our minds to see the importance of faith. It is through faith in Jesus that we "live and move and have our being" (Acts 17:28). It is through this same faith that we experience all that is available in Christ. Everything Jesus died to give us will only become our reality as we apply our faith to God's Word. We are saved by faith, justified by faith, and sanctified by faith. We are able to do all things by faith. We cease from our own labors and enter God's rest by faith. We are empowered by faith. The Holy Spirit lives within us by faith. We overcome sin by faith. We have access to God by faith. We defeat the enemy by faith. We stand by faith. It is through faith that the truths of God's Word become ours. In our homework, we read that it is impossible to please God without faith, that anything that does not stem from faith is sin. As we ponder these passages, they bring an entirely new light to the way we should live. The victorious Christian life will not be experienced apart from faith. Without faith there is no relationship with God. If we desire to participate in the abundant life, faith is of utmost importance.

Just a side note - if you actually looked up all of these verses today, I am really proud of you!!!

On the left of the table below are listed several passages of scripture. To the right is a list of different benefits these scriptures indicate we receive by faith. Match the verse with the benefit received by writing the scripture address beside the item. The first few have been done for you. Remember more than one benefit can be in a verse.

SCRIPTURE

Matthew 9:29
Matthew 17:20
Matthew 21:21-22
Mark 11:22-24
Mark 16:17
John 3:15-16
John 6:47
John 7:38-39
John 14:12
Acts 26:18
Romans 1:5
Romans 3:22
Romans 3:28-30
Romans 4:16
Romans 5:1-2
Romans 10:9-10
2 Corinthians 1:24
Galatians 3:7-9
Galatians 3:14
Galatians 3:26
Ephesians 1:13
Ephesians 1:19
Ephesians 6:16
Philippians 3:9
Hebrews 4:3
Hebrews 11:6

BENEFITS RECEIVED THROUGH FAITH

Salvation/Sonship

Justification

Sanctification

Righteousness

Forgiveness

Ability to please God

Ability to receive and have answered prayer ***Matt. 9:29***

Ability to accomplish things and to do God's work
Matt. 17:20, Matt. 21:21

Enter God's rest

Have the indwelling of the Holy Spirit

Receive power

Ability to obey

Ability to partake of the promises and blessings of Abraham

Ability to have access to God

Ability to not sin

Ability to stand

Ability to defeat the enemy

Day Two

The Truth about Faith

Having established that faith is important, let's turn our attention to the next point. What is faith? According to the Random House Dictionary, faith is "confidence or trust in a person or thing; belief that is not based on proof." According to Hebrews 11:1, faith is, "Being sure of what we hope for and certain of what we do not see." I want to highlight two words in these definitions, the word confidence and the word sure. These two words contain the essence of faith. Faith is not just a hope of something, it is the surety and confidence of it. Faith is an inner "knowing," being absolutely convinced even though there is no proof. Many times faith is confused with hope. Hope is a feeling that something is possible; although wonderful to have, it will never move mountains. Hope does not give us power; faith does. Hope encourages; faith energizes. Hope brings comfort but has no ability to bring about true change. Faith brings the power to change. Faith is not a feeling or an emotion; it is a choice. Faith is making the decision to believe what God says. Many Christians are living a life of hope and calling it faith. For this reason, they are not living in power and victory. If we want to grow out of a life of hoping into a life of faith, we must seek to know the truth and choose to believe it. This is the key to faith.

Faith is choosing to believe without proof. We discussed earlier that faith is required in order to have a relationship with God and experience the abundant life in Christ. This being the case, if you are like me, your first thought is, "I want more faith." If faith is the key to a relationship with God, then it stands to reason we would want more of it. But is this really what we need? How much faith is enough? Luke 17:5-6 records a conversation relating to this very topic that took place between Jesus and His apostles.

> *"The apostles said to the Lord, 'Increase our faith!' 6 He replied, 'If you have faith as small as a mustard seed, you can say to this mulberry tree, 'Be uprooted and planted in the sea,' and it will obey you."*

It is very interesting to me that Jesus didn't expound on how to obtain more faith. He basically told them they didn't need more faith. He pointed out to them that they could do extraordinary things with faith the size of a mustard seed. Surely we all have at least an amount of faith the size of a mustard seed.

Considering this, the greater issue is the **exercising** of our faith. I believe this is the point Jesus was making to His apostles. He was trying to make them understand that they didn't need more faith, they needed to use the faith they already had. As believers, we all have a measure of faith. Just like a muscle, as we exercise our faith it becomes stronger. When we don't exercise our faith, it becomes weaker. In the entire Bible there is not one reference to increasing faith other than the verse we just read. However there are several references to faith being strengthened or to a faith that is weak. Let's look at a few of them. Fill in the blanks as you read the passages.

Acts 16:5

"So the churches were _______________ in the faith and grew daily in numbers."

Romans 4:20

"Yet he did not waver through unbelief regarding the promise of God, but was

___________________ in his faith and gave glory to God"

Colossians 2:7

"rooted and built up in him, _____________________ in the faith as you were taught,

and overflowing with thankfulness."

1 Thessalonians 3:2

"We sent Timothy, who is our brother and God's fellow worker in spreading the gospel

of Christ, to _____________________and encourage you in your faith"

Romans 4:19

"Without _________________ in his faith, he faced the fact that his body was as good as

dead—since he was about a hundred years old—and that Sarah's womb was also dead."

Romans 14:1

"Accept him whose faith is _________, without passing judgment on disputable matters."

Romans 14:2

"One man's faith allows him to eat everything, but another man, whose faith is

____________, eats only vegetables."

We do not need to worry about getting more faith, but need to focus instead on strengthening the faith we already have. We are told in **Romans 10:17**: *"Consequently, faith comes from hearing the message, and the message is heard through the word of Christ."* When we hear the message of salvation, we are given a measure of faith. It is our responsibility to strengthen that faith. We can strengthen our faith or we can weaken it. We strengthen our faith by exercising it in truth. As we choose to believe God's Word over our feelings, our sight, our intellect, our experience, etc., our faith is strengthened. We weaken our faith by either not exercising it at all or by exercising it in the wrong way.

When we choose not to exalt God's Word and instead make our choices based on what we see, feel, think, experience, etc., we are choosing not to exercise our faith. When we try to use our faith to obtain our own agenda, we are exercising it in the wrong way. An example of this would be the "give to get" mentality. Another example of this would be the practice of "name it, claim it." Both of these philosophies are based on false doctrine. There is an element of truth in them, but they are distorted by the motivation behind the practice. When we exercise our faith in these ways, our faith will be weakened, because this type of application of faith will never be empowered by God. It is false, and unless we come into the understanding of our error, we will become disillusioned with God and ultimately weaken our faith in Him.

We must understand that faith is the vehicle by which we participate in Christ. The motivation to strengthen our faith should never be to increase our ability to get our own way, but to strengthen our faith so that we can live a more effective life in Christ and better fulfill the purposes of God in our lives.

As stated earlier, when we receive the message of Jesus, faith is planted in our hearts. It is ours. God doesn't give us more faith as we go along. When we choose to exercise the faith we have, He strengthens it through the power of the Holy Spirit within us.

In the next lesson, we will continue our discussion about faith. Until then, may God grant us the ability to agree with Him and strengthen our faith!

Day Three

Good Stewards of Faith

In the last lesson, we learned that we don't need more faith. We need to strengthen the faith we have already been given when we accepted Christ as our Savior. Many times we are waiting until we feel faith or until something makes sense to us before we operate in God's promises. True faith is lining our will up with God's Word regardless of anything else. When we choose to believe what God says for no other reason than that He said it, we are operating in faith. The power of God will be present to do exactly what He says He will do. Faith isn't a feeling; it is a choice. Often people let how they feel at any given moment be their measurement of the amount of faith they possess. When they feel close to God, they think they have more faith. When they feel discouraged and estranged from God, they think they have less faith. Faith has absolutely nothing to do with emotions and feelings; it has everything to do with God, His Word, and our will. Whether we feel up or down, the "amount" of faith we have is the same. On the other hand, the **strength** of our faith can be measured by the degree that our lives are in agreement with God's Word.

It is important to believe correctly about faith. There is a huge difference between believing we need something we don't have and believing we need to get better at using something we do have. If we believe the former, we are in the position of a victim, passively waiting on God to give us the faith we need. In our thinking, we are helpless until God decides to move. By contrast, if we believe the latter, we are empowered to exercise that which we have already been given by God and to make a real difference in our circumstances.

Fill in the blanks to 2 Peter 1:3.

> *"His divine power _______ ___________ us everything we need for life and godliness through our knowledge of him who called us by his own glory and goodness."*

This verse tells us that God "has given" us everything we need. It does not say He "will give." He has already given us everything we need; this includes our faith.

Although God has given us faith, some people perceive this faith to be power in and of itself. All power belongs to God. Revelation 4:11 says, "*You are worthy, our Lord and God, to receive glory and honor and power, for you created all things, and by your will they were created and have their being.*" Faith in and of itself is not power. God holds the power. Faith is merely the catalyst to which God has said He will respond. We read earlier that without faith it is impossible to please God. God set this standard. As He reveals Himself to us and we respond by placing our faith in that revelation, God honors the faith by sending forth His power. In reality, faith is our response to revelation from God in order to accomplish the purposes of God. As we strengthen our faith through use, we learn a life of dependency.

I want to encourage each of us to become better stewards of the faith we have been given. Let's see what Luke 19:11-26 has to say about this.

How many minas were entrusted to each servant? ______________________________

What was the king's response to the servant who earned ten more minas? ________

____

____

What was His response to the one who earned five more? ____________________

____

____

Was the king pleased with both of them? ______________________________________

Why do you think the king was so displeased with the servant who hid his mina?

____

____

____

There are many applications of this passage of scripture. One is in this discussion of faith. The king gave each servant the same amount of money. The servants were in control of what they did with that money. In the same way, God has given each of His servants the same amount of faith. It is up to us what we do with our faith. If we learn to exercise our faith, we will bear much fruit for our king; if we choose to bury our faith and not use it, we will not.

Let us not forget that there will come a day when we also will stand before our king – Jesus Christ – and give an account for what we have done with our faith (Romans 14:10, 2 Corinthians 5:10). God is good and faithful. He will help us learn to exercise our faith. He will bless and reward each effort we make to strengthen our faith. However, He will not be pleased if we spend our lives hiding it. In the words of the Apostle Paul, "Consider therefore the kindness and sternness of God . . ." (Romans 11:22). God has given each of us the gift of faith and has promised that He will always respond to our faith. This is a very great and precious promise! We should understand the truth about faith and seek to exercise it that it might become strong and unfailing.

Let's close by reading the following passage. [emphasis added]

> *"These have come so that* ***your faith—of greater worth than gold****, which perishes even though refined by fire—may be proved genuine and may result in praise, glory, and honor when Jesus Christ is revealed."*
>
> *1 Peter 1:7*

May our faith be proved genuine and result in . . . !

Day Four

Enemies of Faith - Pt. 1

So far this week, we have talked about the importance of our belief about faith. When we are saved, we are given a measure of faith. We can either strengthen or weaken that faith. Faith is a choice to believe God and His Word. As we choose to believe God and His Word, we strengthen our faith. When we choose not to believe, we weaken it.

For the remainder of this week, we are going to discuss two enemies of faith: doubt and unbelief. Although these words are often used interchangeably, they are rooted in very different conditions. Doubt arises in the absence of God's revealed will. Unbelief arises in the absence of credence given to God Himself. Doubt says, "I believe God can . . . , I'm just not sure that He will . . . " Unbelief says, "I do not believe God can . . . " Doubt and unbelief often look alike, but they stem from different motivations. It is important to discern their differences so that we can effectively overcome them when they are operating in our lives.

In the life of a believer, doubt manifests when we are unsure of God's will in a given situation. We believe God is able to do what He says, but we aren't sure if He will do it for us. In other words, we do not know His **revealed** will.

Let me give you an example. Several years ago I was in an ATV accident. My left leg was severely injured, and we were unsure if it would ever be normal again. I spent about six weeks in bed and another six months in a wheel chair. I was very fretful about my future for the first couple of weeks. I knew from God's Word that He was able to heal me completely, but I wasn't sure He would do it in this case. One day, while I was lying in bed, God spoke to my spirit and told me that I would be well and able to walk again. From that point on, I did not doubt that He would do this for me. All my doubt disappeared. The only difference between the first two weeks and the remainder of my recovery was a revelation of God's will to me.

Revelation is a "knowing" that comes straight from God's heart to ours. It is the key to combating doubt. This type of knowing does not come from just reading the Bible, but by hearing from God in our spirit. We see many things in the Word that we believe, yet doubt can so easily enter our minds. This occurs because we do not personally hear from God for our situations. We may see a promise in scripture, yet it is not living within us until God reveals it to us. The only way to overcome doubt is to have revelation knowledge of the will of God. This only comes through fellowship with God. In order for us to know what God has to say in any situation, we must seek His will in the matter, and then when He gives us His Word on the issue, our faith will arise and doubt will have no place.

I want to clarify that "His Word on the issue" is not always a clear directive. Sometimes God won't give us a clear answer on something, but He will reveal to us that He has it under control. In the case of my leg, He gave me a clear directive – that I was going to be well. At other times in my life, He has merely said, "I'm aware and it's under control." In both instances, faith reigned because I had a revealed word from Him. Doubt is overcome when we hear from God. As stated earlier, the root problem in doubt is not that we do not believe God; rather, we do not know His will in that given instance. Therefore the solution for doubt is to hear from God.

This is not the case with unbelief. To reiterate, unbelief is the result of placing no credence in God Himself. Unbelief arises when we basically do not believe that God is who He says He is or that He can do what He says He can. It's saying, "I know God's Word says...but I think..." If you are a person that, regardless of how many times God has come through, still just can't trust Him and have peace, your root problem is not doubt; it's unbelief. You aren't suffering from not knowing what He wants in a given situation; you are suffering from not believing He is able. You do not believe God. You may believe "in" God, but you do not believe Him. Unbelief will lead you away from God. When we are operating in unbelief, we will not seek God for our answers; we will seek our "truth" from another source. There is only one way to overcome unbelief, and that is to repent of it. Read Mark 9:20-27.

With which of the father's comments did Jesus take exception? _______________

____

When Jesus exposed the father's unbelief, what was the father's response? ______

____

When we find ourselves struggling with unbelief, this must be our response as well, "I do believe; help me overcome my unbelief."

Having established the difference between doubt and unbelief, let's look in scripture at examples of each of these conditions in operation. The first I want to examine is doubt operating in the life of Abraham and how he overcame it. Read the following passages of scripture.

Genesis 12:1-4

Thought: In this passage, God gave Abram general instructions and promised him that ' he would become a great nation. Abram listened to God and obeyed Him. He obviously was not operating in unbelief because He did as God commanded. Note: Abram was seventy-five years old at the time.

Genesis 13:14-18

Thought: In these verses, God renewed His promise to Abram by telling him that the land he beheld would belong to him and his offspring, which would be as numerous as the dust of the earth. Abram built an altar to the Lord.

Genesis 15:1-9

Thought: This scripture records yet another discussion between God and Abram, only this time we see Abram beginning to doubt. He didn't see how all of those promises were going to be, considering the fact that God had given him no children. But he was honest with God and questioned Him, and God answered Abram. Abram believed God. We are told that his belief was credited to him as righteousness.

Genesis 16:1-4, Genesis 16:15-16

Thought: These verses show that ten years have gone by, and God has still not given Abram a child. Abram decided to take matters into his own hands. At that point, Abram was operating in doubt. He didn't stop believing God would do what He said; He just didn't have God's revealed word on how it was to be accomplished. At that point, all Abram had received was God's general promises. Sound familiar?? Abram was eighty-six years old when he had Ishmael, the son of Hagar.

Genesis 17:1-27

Thought: In this passage, God revealed His specific plan to Abram. God established His covenant with Abraham and instituted circumcision. At the beginning, Abram definitely doubted. Look at verse seventeen which tells us, "Abram laughed and said, 'Will a son be born to a man a hundred years old? Will Sarah bear a child at the age of ninety?'" Abram was honest with God about his feelings and questioned the Lord. But God told him that the covenant would be through a son conceived with Sarah. At that point God changed Abram's name to Abraham and Sarai's name to Sarah. We are told in verse twenty-three that on that very day Abraham circumcised his entire household. Abraham believed God as is evidenced by his actions, and from that point on, there was no indication Abraham ever doubted God on the issue of the child of promise again.

Genesis 21:1-5

Thought: This passage presents the promised child. We see that Abraham was one hundred years old. Twenty-five years have passed from the first promise of the child to the culmination of this promise. Although there were times Abraham doubted, he still received the promise of God, because his confidence remained in God.

Even though there were times Abraham could not see how God would bring about His Word, Abraham never ceased to believe God. After God clearly told Abraham that the covenant was to be with the son of Sarah, Abraham did not doubt; the revelation from God eradicated the doubt. In Abraham's case, the problem was never the credence given to God; it was in knowing God's will in the details. Once he knew, the problem of doubt was eliminated. In Genesis chapter twenty-two, we find that Abraham was so convinced God would do what He said, that he was willing to sacrifice Isaac on an altar at God's command. He completely trusted God to be true to His revealed word. He believed God would raise Isaac back to life if necessary. Hebrews 11:19 tells us, "Abraham reasoned that God could raise the dead, and figuratively speaking, he did receive Isaac back from death." In this instance, all doubt was removed as a result of a direct revelation from God.

In the final lesson of this week, we will look at an example of unbelief. See you tomorrow!

Day Five

Enemies of Faith - Pt. 2

In day four of this week, we began a discussion about two enemies of faith, doubt and unbelief. We learned that doubt arises in the absence of God's revealed will, but that unbelief arises in the absence of credence given to God Himself. Doubt says, "I believe God can . . . , I'm just not sure that He will . . . " Unbelief says, "I do not believe God can . . ." We determined that the way to gain victory over doubt is to have the revealed will of God, and that the way to overcome unbelief is to repent of it. We then looked at an example in scripture of doubt operating in the life of Abraham, and how he overcame it upon receiving a revelation from God regarding the details of his situation.

Today, let's look at an example of unbelief – the Israelites.

Read the following passages of scripture.

Exodus 3:7-10

> **Thought:** These verses record God's promise to rescue the Israelites from the hand of the Egyptians.

Exodus 4:29-31

> **Thought:** In this passage the Israelites heard and believed the Word of the Lord.

Exodus 6:2-9

> **Thought:** This passage once again tells of God's promises to the Children of Israel. Exodus chapter five tells how Moses had gone to Pharaoh and told him what God had said. As a result, Pharaoh increased the hardship upon the Israelites, and the Israelites became angry with Moses for causing them more trouble. In chapter six, verse nine, we see the beginning of the root problem of the Israelites, unbelief. This verse tells us they would not listen to Moses because they were discouraged and under cruel bondage. This goes beyond doubt because they basically did not believe God. They weren't just unsure of how He was going to accomplish His promises; they didn't believe His promises.

Exodus 12:1-42

Thought: After a series of supernatural plagues upon the Egyptians, Exodus chapters seven through eleven record God fulfilling His promise to bring the Israelites out of Egypt. At that point, the Israelites were full of rejoicing and were obedient to God.

Exodus 14:10-31

Thought: This is the story of God parting the Red Sea. God had just led the Israelites victoriously out of Egypt. Notice how quickly they turned on Moses when faced with a problem. But God did a mighty miracle and saved them all. In the last verse of this passage of scripture, we are told the people feared the Lord and put their trust in Him. The Israelites were beginning to develop a pattern of rejoicing when God did something great, but turning against Him at the first sign of trouble.

Exodus 16:1-15

Thought: The Israelites became hungry in the desert and once again turned on God and Moses. God heard their cry and brought them quail and manna.

Exodus 17:1-7

Thought: This is another situation in which the Israelites murmured and complained against God, and He provided for their needs.

Exodus 32:1, 32:7-14

Thought: Moses had gone up and met with God on Mount Sinai. He was there forty days. During that time, the Israelites completely rejected God and began to worship a golden calf that Aaron had made, even to the point of giving the idol credit for bringing them up out of Egypt. Forty days! My goodness! It didn't take them long to turn, yet God had mercy and did not destroy all of them.

Numbers 11:1-3

Thought: Here is another example of the Israelites murmuring against God. This time God sent a fire to destroy some of them until Moses prayed and asked Him to relent.

Numbers 13:1-3, 13:21, 13:26-33, 14:1-24

Thought: These scriptures tell of the final act of unbelief that cost the Israelites their promised land. They acted in unbelief time after time with no apparent consequence, but this time it cost them their promise from God. Just as God said, not one of them except Joshua and Caleb got to enter the Promised Land.

We see over and over again the children of Israel refusing to believe God and trust Him. He repeatedly saved and provided for them, but they could not seem to trust Him. Every time something went wrong, they cried to go back to the land of their slavery. Because of their unbelief, they never received the promise of God. They died in the desert. These people were not struggling with doubt; they just flat out did not believe God, and they refused to take Him at His Word. God gave them many opportunities to repent but they would not. Unbelief cost them their promise from God.

Unbelief will lead us to disobedience and rebellion and will result in our not receiving the promises of God. Fill in the blanks to the following passages of scripture.

Hebrews 3:16-19

> *"Who were they who heard and rebelled? Were they not all those Moses led out of Egypt? 17 And with whom was he angry for forty years? Was it not with those who sinned, whose bodies fell in the desert? 18 And to whom did God swear that they would never enter his rest if not to those who disobeyed? 19 So we see that they were not able to enter,* ____________________ ________ ____________ ____________."

Hebrew 4:1-2

> *"Therefore, since the promise of entering his rest still stands, let us be careful that none of you be found to have fallen short of it. 2 For we also have had the gospel preached to us, just as they did; but the message they heard was of no value to them, because those who heard did not* __________________ _______ __________ ______________."

Doubt is a condition that comes when we don't have a revealed word of God. Unbelief comes when a person doesn't have confidence in God, His abilities, or His Word. Doubt will make us "blown and tossed by every wind and wave" (James 1:6). Unbelief will lead us away from God. Doubt will not cost us the promises of God; unbelief will. Christians can operate in both of these conditions. The cure for doubt is maturity. The cure for unbelief is repentance.

We all struggle or have struggled with doubt and unbelief. God has the answer for both. When we doubt, we should seek God more and learn to hear His voice. If we will press into God and not grow weary (Hebrews 12:3), we will gain the victory over doubt. We will mature in the Lord and learn to hear His revealed word. Then our faith will rise to the occasion. When struggling with unbelief, we must repent and ask God to forgive us and help us overcome our unbelief. Then we need to begin to make decisions that lead us toward God.

Both doubt and unbelief war against our faith. As we learned earlier this week, faith is the foundation of our entire Christian experience. We must learn to discern the presence of doubt and unbelief, understand which is which, and exercise our weapons against them. As I say in almost every lesson, God is faithful and will help us!

Let's close by reading Hebrews12:2. [emphasis added]

> *"Let us fix our eyes on Jesus, the* **author and perfecter of our faith***, who for the joy set before him endured the cross, scorning its shame, and sat down at the right hand of the throne of God."*

WEEK SIX

MAIN CONCEPTS

DAY 1: WHAT IS FREEDOM

DAY 2: OUR RIGHTS OF FREE CHOICE

DAY 3: OUR RIGHTS OF CITIZENSHIP

DAY 4: WE HAVE BEEN GIVEN FREEDOM

DAY 5: ASCERTAINING OUR LEVEL OF FREEDOM

Day One

Exemption from External Control

"It is for freedom that Christ has set us free . . ."

Galatians 5:1

In our final two weeks of this study, we are going to examine our beliefs about freedom. Few believers, if any, are living in the freedom that is available to us. We are told in scripture that Jesus has set us free . . . for freedom. What exactly does this mean? What is freedom and how do we obtain it? How are we to know if we are free? If we feel free, does that mean we are free? We are going to address these questions and a few more as we study the concept of freedom.

Freedom is such a broad subject that, truthfully, it is somewhat intimidating to try to expound on. However, through the empowerment of the Holy Spirit, I am going to try to share insights about freedom that will, hopefully, enable us to live in its reality more and more. Our study of freedom is going to be separated into two segments. In the first segment, we will try to answer the question, "What is freedom?" In the second, we will address the question, "How do we obtain it?"

Everyone wants freedom. However, if we were to ask a thousand people what freedom means to them, we would get a thousand different answers. Some of the responses might be

- not having someone tell me what to do
- having all the money I need
- not having cancer
- being thin
- having arms
- not being in an abusive relationship

To many, freedom represents deliverance from a particular thing that has them bound. But true freedom is so much more. Freedom is a state of being; a condition. There are always two connotations to it: freedom from and freedom to. In other words, when we are truly free, we are equally: free from . . . in order to be free to . . . . We want to be **free from** having someone tell us what to do, so that we are **free to** do what we want, and so on.

Freedom is not a state of nothingness; it is a state of enablement. In every area that we gain freedom, we are delivered from something while simultaneously being enabled to something else.

Having introduced this concept, let's take a look at the definition of the term freedom taken from the Random House Dictionary.

- the state of being free or at liberty rather than in confinement or under physical restraint
- exemption from external control, interference, regulation, etc.
- the power to determine action without restraint
- personal liberty, as opposed to bondage or slavery: a slave who bought his freedom
- exemption from the presence of anything specified (usually fol. by from): freedom from fear.
- the right to enjoy all the privileges or special rights of citizenship, membership, etc., in a community or the like

Philosophy: the power to exercise choice and make decisions without constraint from within or without; autonomy; self-determination

Synonyms: liberty, opportunity, right, leeway

For the purposes of this lesson, we are going to examine in detail four main components of freedom taken from the above definition. They are:

1. exemption from external control
2. the power to exercise choice
3. the right to enjoy all the privileges or special rights of citizenship
4. exemption from the presence of

Exemption from External Control

The first element in the definition of freedom states that freedom is the condition of being exempt from external control. This seems to conflict with Christian theology. If you asked most Christians, "Does God want to be in control of you?" they would answer, "Yes!" But does He? Let's look into the Word and see.

Read the following passages

Galatians 5:22-23

Thought: The fruit of the Spirit listed in this passage are not things we try to obtain; they are things that become apparent in our lives as a result of the presence of the Holy Spirit.

What is the last fruit listed in verse 23? ________________________________

Ephesians 4:21-24

Who is putting off the old self and putting on the new? **Circle one:** You God

Colossians 3:8-10

What can you infer from this passage about who is in control of you? ____________________

____

2 Timothy 1:7

This scripture tells us that God "did not give us a spirit of timidity, but a spirit of power, love

and" what kind of discipline? ____________________

Titus 1:7-9, Titus 2:2-12, 2 Peter 1:5-7

How many times do we find the term "self-controlled" in these passages? ________

Girls, God does not want to control us! He wants us to control ourselves. Satan, on the other hand, **does** want to control us. He does not want us to exercise control over ourselves; he wants us to give that control to him. God does not want to usurp our will; Satan does. When Adam and Eve sinned, they gave up their God-given authority. Satan knew if he could get them to go against God, he could enslave them. They did and he did. God had given Adam and Eve authority over all of His creation, including themselves. Read Genesis 1:26-31.

Who was to rule over all of God's creation? ______________________________

When did God give them this authority? ______________________________

When Adam and Eve believed the serpent and disobeyed God, they gave their authority over to Satan. This is what Paul is talking about in Romans 8:19-21. [emphasis added]

"The creation waits in eager expectation for the sons of God to be revealed. 20 ***For the creation was subjected to frustration, not by its own choice, but by the will of the one who subjected it,*** *in hope 21 that the creation itself will be liberated from its bondage to decay and brought into the freedom and glory of the children of God."*

This can also be seen in Luke 4:5-7. [emphasis added]

"The devil led him up to a high place and showed him in an instant all the kingdoms of the world. 6 And he said to him, 'I will give you all their authority and splendor, ***for it has been given to me****, and I can give it to anyone I want to. 7 So if you worship me, it will all be yours.' "*

Adam and Eve gave their authority over to Satan. Now all of man and all of creation are in bondage to Satan. They didn't give Satan their will, but they did give him their authority. Satan can't make man do anything, but, in essence, the unregenerated man is unable to exercise authority over Satan. In an unsaved person, the sin nature reigns. Christ came to enable man to take back that authority. This is accomplished through faith in Him. Matthew 28:18 says,

> *"Then Jesus came to them and said, "All authority in heaven and on earth has been given to me."*

Luke 10:18-19 says,

> *"He replied, 'I saw Satan fall like lightning from heaven. 19 I have given you authority to trample on snakes and scorpions and to overcome all the power of the enemy; nothing will harm you.'"*

When Jesus died on the cross, He, in essence, purchased back our rightful position. He redeemed us. Read the following verses and fill in the blanks.

Revelation 5:9

> *"And they sang a new song, saying: 'You are worthy to take the scroll and to*
>
> *open its seals, because you were slain, and with your blood you* _____________
>
> _______ _____ ________ *from every tribe and language and people and nation.'"*

1 Peter 1:18

> *"For you know that it was not with perishable things such as silver or gold that*
>
> *you were* __________________ *from the empty way of life* ________________
>
> __________ _____ _______ *from your* ______________________,"

Luke 1:68

> *"Praise be to the Lord, the God of Israel, because he has come and has*
>
> _______________*His people."*

When we accept Christ as our savior, we receive much more than just escape from hell. We receive back the authority that was rightfully ours to begin with. Satan has no authority in the life of a believer unless we give it to him. We discussed this in detail in week three. Because of the price that Jesus paid, we are free once again to fulfill our original purpose. We are free to not have to sin. Before salvation, we are not able to stop sinning; we are born sinners. I've said before that we are not sinners because we sin; we sin because we are sinners. Pre-salvation, we are in bondage to our sin nature which is under the authority of Satan. Upon salvation, however, we are no longer bound by the sin nature and are free to stop sinning. We are free from the authority of Satan and are once again free to be in control of ourselves. As stated earlier, if we are free from something, it is in order for us to be free to something else. Therefore, since Christ has freed us from external control, it is to enable us to be in control of ourselves.

We will discuss what we do with our control a little later on. For now, let's just say that the first element of freedom is to be free from external control. We have this through faith in the finished work of Jesus Christ.

Day Two

Power to Exercise Choice

In the last lesson, we began our discussion of freedom. We talked about the first element in its definition. Jesus Christ has set us free from the external control of Satan and enabled us to have the ability to be self-controlled. Let's move on to the next element.

Power to Exercise Choice

The definition of freedom states that freedom is also the power to exercise choice. This element completely dovetails with exemption from external control. If we are free from external control, then we have been empowered to exercise our choice, the from/to principle again. A main theme throughout this study has been the effect of our choices on our lives. Christ purchased our freedom; therefore, we have the ability to choose any path we want. Notice the first element did not say we were exempt from external **influence** but from **control**. Influence plays a key role in this second element of freedom. Once we belong to Christ, Satan knows he has lost his authority over us; therefore, he works overtime in the area of influence. He knows just how free we are, and he diligently tries to convince us that nothing has changed. If we do not recognize this, we will not be on guard against his schemes. Satan knows that when we are armed with the truth of our purchased freedom, we are extremely dangerous to his agenda. He works to make sure we become convinced that we are, in fact, not free. As we have learned over and over again, if we believe his lies, we will then make the very choices that will lead us back into the bondage we are escaping. Let me give you a practical example of what this might look like in the life of a believer.

Suppose you are an unsaved alcoholic. You have been told for years that alcoholism is a disease and that you can never really be free from it. You believe that the best you can hope for is to somehow learn to control this sickness. Let's say that one of your co-workers, who happens to be a Christian, invites you to a retreat, and while you are there, you hear the message of salvation. For the first time in years there is a burning hope within your heart that maybe, just maybe, you really can be different. You take the plunge and accept Christ as your savior. From that moment you are, in fact, set free from the authority of Satan to control you by your addiction to alcohol.

Satan is very aware that you are free, but he is banking that he can convince you otherwise. If he can cause you to believe, through feelings, experiences, people, etc., that you are not free, then you will make the choices that will lead you to give ground back to him. You will become entangled once again in the bondage of alcoholism.

In order to partake of the freedom that is rightfully ours, we must, through belief and choice, participate in that freedom. In the spiritual realm, your freedom is a reality. However, in order for us to benefit from that reality, we must actively apply the truth to our lives every day. We do this by believing what God says and letting that belief dictate our choices.

Satan wants to defeat us in our minds and use the influence of his lies to take control of our choices. God wants to empower us with truth that we might be free to choose to believe Him. If we do so, we will live free.

Write John 8:32 in the space below.

Read Hebrews 2:14-15.

What did the death of Jesus destroy? ________________________________

____

Read Luke 4:18.

According to this verse, God has sent Jesus to proclaim what to the prisoner? __________

____

And to do what for the oppressed? ______________________________

John 8:36 says, "*So if the Son sets you free, you will be free indeed.*" Jesus Christ has set us free. We are in total control of our choices which will either lead us to exercise the freedom we have been given or lead us back under the power of Satan. Christ has enabled us to exercise our free choice, but it's up to us what we do with that freedom. As Christians, we can choose what we are or are not going to do every day. We have that right! Praise be to Jesus!

Day Three

The Privileges of Citizenship

Right to Enjoy all the Privileges or Special Rights of Citizenship

The third element of freedom is to have the right to enjoy all the privileges or special rights of citizenship. When Christ came, he came with a kingdom. There are multiple references to this kingdom in the New Testament. Let's look at a few of them.

[emphasis added]

Luke 1:30–33

> *"But the angel said to her, 'Do not be afraid, Mary, you have found favor with God. 31 You will be with child and give birth to a son, and you are to give him the name Jesus. 32 He will be great and will be called the Son of the Most High. The Lord God will give him the throne of his father David, 33 and he will reign over the house of Jacob forever;* ***his kingdom*** *will never end.'"*

Matthew 3:1-2

> *"In those days John the Baptist came, preaching in the Desert of Judea 2 and saying, 'Repent, for the* **kingdom of heaven** *is near.'"*

Matthew 4:17

> *"From that time on Jesus began to preach, 'Repent, for* **the kingdom of heaven** *is near.'"*

Matthew 5:20

> *"For I tell you that unless your righteousness surpasses that of the Pharisees and the teachers of the law, you will certainly not enter the* **kingdom of heaven.**"

Acts 1:3

"After his suffering, he showed himself to these men and gave many convincing proofs that he was alive. He appeared to them over a period of forty days and spoke about the ***kingdom of God.****"*

Mark 1:15

"'The time has come,' he said. 'The ***kingdom of God*** *is near. Repent and believe the good news!'"*

Through faith in Jesus, we have the right to participate in this kingdom. The Word tells us that we are heirs and co-heirs with Christ (Romans 8:17). This means that we have the right of citizenship in the kingdom of God. Several verses in the Bible speak of this. Let's look at a few.

Luke 12:32

What has the Father been pleased to give us? ______________________________

Luke 22:28-30

What has Christ conferred on us? ______________________________________

Hebrews 12:28

Who is receiving a kingdom that cannot be shaken? ________________________

James 2:5

To whom does God promise the kingdom? _______________________________

Ephesians 2:18-20

What does verse 19 tell us we are? ____________________________________

____

How do we have access to this citizenship and this household? ______________

____

Who is the chief cornerstone? ____

Luke 17:20-21

According to these verses, where is the kingdom of God? __________________

Through faith in Jesus Christ, we are citizens in the kingdom of God. And through this same faith we have all the rights of citizenship. Let's list some of those rights.

- access to the Father – oneness with God
- protection

"I pray for them. I am not praying for the world, but for those you have given me, for they are yours. 10 All I have is yours, and all you have is mine. And glory has come to me through them. 11 I will remain in the world no longer, but they are still in the world, and I am coming to you. Holy Father, protect them by the power of your name, the name you gave me, so that they may be one as we are one."

John 17:9-11

- the glory of Jesus

"Father, I want those you have given me to be with me where I am, and to see my glory, the glory you have given me because you loved me before the creation of the world."

John 17:24

- no condemnation

"Therefore, there is now no condemnation for those who are in Christ Jesus,"

Romans 8:1

- authority over the enemy

"I have given you authority to trample on snakes and scorpions and to overcome all the power of the enemy; nothing will harm you."

Luke 10:19

- promises of God's Word

"For no matter how many promises God has made, they are 'Yes' in Christ. And so through him the 'Amen' is spoken by us to the glory of God."

2 Corinthians 1:20

- secrets of the kingdom

"He replied, 'The knowledge of the secrets of the kingdom of heaven has been given to you, but not to them.'"

Matthew 13:11

- keys to the kingdom

"I will give you the keys of the kingdom of heaven; whatever you bind on earth will be bound in heaven, and whatever you loose on earth will be loosed in heaven."

Matthew 16:19

• abundant life

> *"The thief comes only to steal and kill and destroy; I have come that they may have life, and have it to the full."*
>
> *John 10:10*

This is by no means a comprehensive list of the rights of citizenship in the kingdom of God, but just a few of the things that we have been given in Christ. When we accept Christ as our savior, we enter the kingdom of God. It is through faith that we have the right to enjoy all the privileges of citizenship.

Day Four

Exemption from the Presence Of

Today, we are going to discuss the final element in our definition of freedom. We have already learned that when we are free we will have exemption from external control, the right to exercise choice, and the right to enjoy all the privileges or special rights of citizenship. Let's see what else we enjoy when we walk in freedom.

Exemption from the Presence Of

The final element of freedom according to our definition is exemption from the presence of. In the definition we previously read, it was stated as follows.

> *"exemption from the presence of anything specified (usually fol. by from): freedom from fear."*

Through our participation in Christ, we are free from anything that would set itself up against the knowledge and the Word of God.

Fill in the blanks of 2 Corinthians 10:5.

> *"We ____________________ arguments and every pretension that sets itself up against the knowledge of God, and we ____________ ______________ every thought to make it obedient to Christ."*

We have a God-given right to say no to anything that is not in agreement with God. What would this include? Basically, anything that limits us. Freedom from:

- fear
- insecurity
- anger and bitterness
- depression
- lying
- lust and sexual perversion
- addiction
- obesity
- unforgiveness
- eating disorders
- greed
- obsessions

The list could go on and on. All of these spring from the sin nature. The Words tells us that we have been set free from sin. Look up Romans 6:18 and write it in the space below.

We have been set free from sin and therefore, regardless of what we are told, we do not have to stay in bondage to anything. Jesus Christ paid a very high price and redeemed us from the fall. Through faith we have everything the Word of God says is ours. Appropriating these promises into our lives isn't easy; it takes guts and determination. I love what Matthew 11:12 says about the type of people who are going to participate in the kingdom of God. Fill in the blanks to this verse.

> *"From the days of John the Baptist until now, the kingdom of heaven has been*
>
> *forcefully advancing, and ____________ men lay hold of it."*

We will discuss this more later. For now, suffice it to say, we have been given the right to be free from anything and everything that does not line up with God and His Word, but this will not be our reality unless we become forceful about it.

We began our discussion of freedom with Galatians 5:1, which says, "It is for freedom that Christ has set us free . . . ." The questions were asked, "What exactly does this mean?" and "What is freedom?" True freedom can only be found in and through Jesus Christ. He lived, died, and rose again to redeem anyone that will choose to place his or her faith in Him. When we do so, we are given freedom. We are given exemption from external control in order that we might be self-controlled. We are given the power to exercise our choice and the right to enjoy the privileges of citizenship in the kingdom of God. Finally, we are given exemption from anything that sets itself up against the knowledge of God. **This is freedom!**

I want to challenge each of us to ask, "Am I living in the freedom that is rightfully mine?" If not, we must keep pressing on until we are living in the reality of the truth of God. God has made a way; let's take it!

Day Five

Are We Free?

So far this week, we have discussed the definition of freedom. Beginning in this lesson, we are going to examine how to appropriate our God-given freedom; in other words, how to make this freedom our reality.

The Word of God tells us,

"It is for freedom that Christ has set us free. . . "

Galatians 5:1

Notice in this verse we are not told that Christ **will** set us free; we are told that he already has. Let's look at a few more verses in scripture that tell us the same thing.

Fill in the blanks.

Romans 6:6-7

> *"For we know that our old self was crucified with him so that the body of sin might be done away with that we should no longer be slaves to sin 7) because anyone who has died ________ _________ _______ from sin."*

Romans 8:2

> *"because through Christ Jesus the law of the Spirit of life _____ ______ _______ from the law of sin and death."*

Colossians 1:22

> *"But now he ________ reconciled you by Christ's physical body through death to present you holy in his sight, without blemish, and free from accusation"*

Revelation 1:5

> *"and from Jesus Christ, who is the faithful witness, the firstborn from the dead, and the ruler of the kings of the earth. To him who loves us and ______ freed us from our sins by his blood,"*

In each of these verses, freedom is a past tense condition which means our freedom has already been provided. Christ paid the price, and freedom is ours. This being the case, are we free?

Let's take a few moments and ascertain our level of freedom. Only God can truly know where we are absolutely free and where we are not. However, I believe it is beneficial to take stock of ourselves. In 2 Corinthians 13:5 we are told to examine ourselves. In this lesson we are going to do so in light of the definition of freedom. Answer the following questions as honestly as you can. Only in total honesty is this exercise beneficial.

• Exemption from External Control

1. I live a self-controlled life.	always	often	rarely	never
2. I am **not** easily manipulated by others.	always	often	rarely	never
3. When someone does something wrong to me, I can give it to God and let it go.	always	often	rarely	never
4. I spend much of every day at peace with others.	always	often	rarely	never
5. My mind is free from negative emotions.	always	often	rarely	never
6. I do what I know is right, regardless of what I feel.	always	often	rarely	never
7. I always say what I should.	always	often	rarely	never

• The power to exercise choice

1. When I know I have had enough to eat or drink, I stop.	always	often	rarely	never
2. When I know something is harmful, I avoid it.	always	often	rarely	never
3. I carry out my decisions, e.g. I am going to clean my house today.	always	often	rarely	never
4. I know the truth of God's Word and make my decisions accordingly.	always	often	rarely	never
5. I know what I want.	always	often	rarely	never
6. I make up my mind about things.	always	often	rarely	never
7. I am not easily swayed.	always	often	rarely	never

• The right to enjoy all the privileges of citizenship in the kingdom of God

1. I enjoy the presence of God.	always	often	rarely	never
2. I am free from the feelings of condemnation for my sins and failures.	always	often	rarely	never
3. I exercise my authority over Satan.	always	often	rarely	never
4. I am living in the promises of God's Word.	always	often	rarely	never
5. I participate in the glory of Jesus.	always	often	rarely	never
6. I am living the abundant life.	always	often	rarely	never
7. I am growing and learning new insights about God every day.	always	often	rarely	never
8. I live in much joy.	always	often	rarely	never
9. I live in much peace.	always	often	rarely	never
10. I am doing even greater things than Jesus did. *(John 14:12)*	always	often	rarely	never

• Exemption from anything that sets itself up against the knowledge of God

1. I am free from fear.	always	often	rarely	never
2. I know my God has good things for me.	always	often	rarely	never
3. I know God will make all things work for my good.	always	often	rarely	never
4. I am free from depression.	always	often	rarely	never
5. I am free from insecurity.	always	often	rarely	never
6. I am free from addiction.	always	often	rarely	never
7. I am free from obesity.	always	often	rarely	never
8. I am free from anger, bitterness, & unforgiveness.	always	often	rarely	never
9. I am free from lying.	always	often	rarely	never
10. I am free from greed.	always	often	rarely	never
11. I am free from lust and sexual perversion.	always	often	rarely	never
12. I am free from eating disorders.	always	often	rarely	never
13. I am free from obsessions.	always	often	rarely	never
14. I am free from feelings of guilt.	always	often	rarely	never
15. I am content.	always	often	rarely	never
16. I believe God.	always	often	rarely	never
17. I know I am precious to God and He delights in me.	always	often	rarely	never

Now, let's tally our answers.

How many items were circled in each column? ______ ______ ______ ______

What can we glean about ourselves from this exercise? Well, if you circled always every time, then you are either perfected in Christ and ready to move on out of here or you are a terrible liar. Ha! I doubt any of us circle *always* every time. In all seriousness, I'm sure every one of us has a number in each of the above blanks. Here is the best way to interpret the exercise we have just completed. If you have a high number in the *always* and *often* columns, then you are probably living in a good bit of freedom. If you have higher numbers in the *rarely* and *never* columns, more than likely you are not living in very much freedom.

This is merely a tool used to give us an indication of our level of freedom. It's certainly not exact and is not intended to puff up or discourage. However, if we want to live in the freedom that is rightfully ours, we must ascertain our need for it. I asked the question in the last lesson, "If we feel free, does that mean we are?" The answer to this question is "No!" Just because we think we are free does not mean we are. Some of the most bound people I know would say they are the most free. Look at the Jews in John 8:31-34. They actually told Jesus they had never been slaves of anyone. They were under Roman rule at the time. They had been slaves time and time again, all through their history, because of their unfaithfulness to God.

Some Christians know they are living in bondage because they see the fruit of it every day. Others think they are living in freedom when, in fact, they are not. Self-righteous, religious people are an example of this. They have a tendency to think that because they go to a particular church or obey a particular set of rules, they are living in freedom. However, they are not participating in the fullness of the Spirit. They completely miss the fact that they are in bondage to pride, which is the very root of the sin nature.

Often we are bound by things handed down to us from our parents. We don't recognize these things as bondage because they feel so normal to us. Most children born and raised in slavery do not have a concept of freedom. Therefore, they don't seek it. Many Christians have been born and raised in spiritual slavery, and do not realize their bondage. Satan has built layer upon layer of false doctrine and lies in their hearts and minds, and they do not even realize they are bound. These people have no concept of the freedom that is rightfully theirs. If you are bound in this way, you don't know it. You don't think you are in bondage, but that doesn't mean you are not. Bound people are blind people.

We are only free when we are living in what God defines as freedom. The way we can know whether we are free or not is by examining how closely our lives agree with the Word of God. The above exercise highlighted a few things the Word says are the fruit of freedom, but, as stated earlier, it is not an all inclusive test. God's Word is our final exam. If our lives reflect the truth of the Word, then we are living in freedom. Said another way, to whatever degree we are exalting God's Word in our daily lives, it is to this same degree that we are experiencing freedom.

WEEK SEVEN

MAIN CONCEPTS

DAY 1: BONDAGE IS THE RESULT OF SIN

DAY 2: EXAMINING OUR LIVES IN THE LIGHT OF THE WORD

DAY 3: LEARNING TO HEAR THE HOLY SPIRIT IN MAKING CHOICES

DAY 4: HOLDING ON TO OUR VICTORIES

DAY 5: REAPING A HARVEST

Day One

Bondage: The Result of Sin

Last week, we discussed the definition of freedom and defined our personal need for it. This week, let's turn our attention to how to participate more fully in the freedom we have been given.

Regardless of our level of freedom, each of us could stand to live more free. How do we do this? First, we have to recognize that all bondage (the opposite of freedom) is the result of sin. As we discussed last week, the general bondage of mankind is the result of the sin of Adam and Eve. The specific, individual bondage we each have also stems from sin. It is not always the product of our own sin, but it will be the result of some form of sin. For the purposes of this lesson, I want to further divide the root of sin into four categories:

- Disobedience
- Ignorance
- Unbelief
- Imposed

All bondage is the result of one of the four things listed above. Let's take a closer look at each of them.

Disobedience

Some of our bondage will be the result of pure disobedience. When there is a clear directive in the Word of God, but we ignore it, we are exercising disobedience. This type of sin comes in two forms, the sin of omission or the sin of commission. The sin of omission occurs when we know what we are supposed to do and don't do it. An example of a bondage resulting from this type of disobedience might be bitterness. The root of bitterness is unforgiveness, and the Word clearly tells us we have to forgive those who have wronged us (Mark 11:25, Luke 6:37, Luke 17:4). When we refuse to forgive, a root of bitterness grows in our hearts. The sin of commission occurs when we know what we are **not** supposed to do but do it anyway. An example of a bondage resulting from this type of disobedience might be the bondage we would suffer in a marriage to a non-believer. In 2 Corinthians 6:14 we are plainly told not to be yoked together with unbelievers. But when we are young and in love, we are just sure we can convince Mr. Wonderful to get saved and serve God. Therefore, we completely disregard the Word of God and do what we want. The outcome is bondage. The cure for bondage rooted in the sin of disobedience is repentance.

Ignorance

Some of our bondage will be the result of pure ignorance. We don't know what the Bible says; therefore, we do not know what we should do. We just do what seems right to us, and the result is bondage. Write Proverbs 14:12 in the space below.

There are times when our ignorance costs us dearly. An example of this might be the bondage of having children who are out of control. In case you are unaware, this is a terrible bondage. There is so much propaganda circulating in our culture today regarding the proper way to rear children. It is often said that disciplining our children will somehow warp them and ruin their self-image. I'm very sad to say there are many Christians totally ignorant of the fact that God's Word tells us to discipline our children, "for in that there is hope" (Proverbs 19:18). Several other verses in the Bible speak more specifically about discipline; however, we won't get into that today. The point is, if we are unaware that God says to be careful to discipline our children, then we will fall for all the garbage that "makes sense." This will produce bondage, not only in our own soul, but also in the souls of our children. Bondage arising from ignorance comes from not knowing God and His Word, and can be removed by getting into the Word and asking God for wisdom.

Unbelief

At times we are in bondage because we are consumed with doubt and unbelief. An example of this might be the bondage of fear. Fear, in this sense, is a controlling fear that might grip our lives in a given area; e.g., the fear of losing a child, of staying by yourself at night, of rejection. Any type of phobia would fall under this bondage. This type of fear, as opposed to a normal fear, e.g., the fear that would occur if someone were holding a gun to your head, is the result of unbelief. If we are bound by this type of fear, then we basically do not believe God loves us. In 1 John 4:18 we are told that "There is no fear in love. But perfect love drives out fear, because fear has to do with punishment. The one who fears is not made perfect in love." God tells us throughout His Word that He loves us. Therefore the bondage of fear stems from unbelief, not believing God loves us. These types of bondage can be broken by repenting, maturing in the Lord, and crying out, "Help me overcome my unbelief" (Mark 9:24).

Imposed

Certain types of bondage are imposed upon us by things that are outside of our control. These bondages result from the sin of someone else, such as a parent or husband. These are often the most painful kind of bondages and the most difficult to overcome. An example would be bondage originating from childhood abuse. As a child, you cannot control your parents' harmful behavior and are helpless to do anything about your situation. Because of this, you may grow up with a horrible inferiority complex or an obsessive need to be in control. Many types of bondage are imposed upon us because they are passed from one generation to the next. A few examples of this might be ignorance, poverty, alcoholism, or paranoia. The defining feature of an imposed bondage is that, at its origin, the individual did not have a choice. The bondage was imposed by another.

As previously mentioned, imposed bondage is the most difficult to break, for in these types of bondage there exists a strong element of justification. For instance, if you have the bondage of having to be in control, your mind immediately begins to defend your behavior any time the Holy Spirit brings conviction. It pulls from your victimization causing strong feelings to emerge from what you have experienced, making your behavior appear just. Your thoughts might go something like this, "I know the Word tells me to submit to my husband, but if I do, it will give him power to take advantage of me." Imposed bondage is very serious and takes a supernatural healing from God to overcome.

As stated earlier, all bondage is a result of sin, whether it be disobedience, ignorance, unbelief, or a sin imposed upon us. Recognizing the root of bondage will make us more effective in breaking free.

Day Two

The General Path to Freedom - LIBERTY

In the last lesson, we learned that all bondage is the result of sin. It is not always the result of our own sin, but it will be the result of sin in some form. I would love to say that we each have only one major bondage and that once we figure out what it is and defeat it, we are free from then on. This simply is not the case. Bondage is anything less than perfect freedom; therefore, we all have much bondage to overcome. Regardless of the root of our bondage, there are certain general steps we must take in order to break free. Within those general steps, there are certain specific things we will do depending on the root of the bondage. Though we will all follow the same path in obtaining freedom, we will wear different shoes while walking that path, depending on the bondage. For the sake of this lesson, I am going to call the general path LIBERTY.

L – Look and examine
I – Implore and petition
B – Be attentive and listen
E – Exercise choice
R – Recognize and Regard
T – Take our stand
Y – Yield our crop

Let's take a closer look at each one.

L – Look and Examine

The first step in breaking free from any bondage is to look at and examine our lives. As I asked earlier, if we don't know we are bound, how can we go free? Read the following verses and answer the questions.

1 Corinthians 11:31

What does this verse imply we should do? ________________________________

2 Corinthians 13:5

What does this verse tell us to do? ________________________________

Scripture tells us to examine ourselves. We begin this process by asking God to show us the truth about ourselves. More than likely, we are blind in the areas of our bondage, and it is going to take the Holy Spirit to reveal the truth to us in these areas. Our prayer for this might be, "Dear Father, I know there are areas in my life where I am not living in the freedom that is rightfully mine. I ask you to open my eyes to see the area(s) of bondage you would like me to deal with. Protect me from the enemy and his lies, and help me to know the truth that I might live free. Please give me the courage to face myself. Thank you, Lord Jesus!" I promise that God will begin to highlight areas in your life that do not line up with His Word.

An example of revealed bondage in my life is in the area of my relationship with my 13-year-old son. Don't you dare laugh! Yes, I thought I would be different from all you other moms. Ha! Ha! When I examine my life in this area, I see a lot of contention, anxiety, lack of peace, and stress. I can see that this does not line up with the Word of God. I know God's Word tells me that I should live at peace with all men, be anxious for nothing, and have the peace that passes all understanding. This is not what I am currently experiencing. Therefore, I know there is an element of bondage in this area of my life. Remember, there are levels of bondage. There is deep, long-term, very debilitating bondage, and there is less debilitating and not so dramatic bondage. Mine is an example of the latter. However, it is still keeping me from living in total freedom. I could discuss other areas, such as self control in eating, being a people pleaser, and believing God for my future, but I think this particular one will work well as we walk through these steps toward freedom. I want each of you to know that I had my son read this and have only used us as an example with his blessing. He really is a great kid; he's just 13 and my first, if you know what I mean. ☺

Okay, back to the subject. The Bible is our measuring rod of freedom. Earlier we did an exercise that helped us ascertain our level of freedom in a general sense. Following are a few scriptures that can be used to measure our freedom in more specific ways.

- Matthew 6
- Matthew 7:1-5
- Mark 8:34-35
- Romans 8:1-2
- Romans 12:9-21
- 1 Corinthians 13:4-7
- Galatians 5:22-26
- Ephesians 4:29-32
- Philippians 2:14-15
- Philippians 3:13-14
- Philippians 4:4-8
- Colossians 2:6-23
- Colossians 3:12-25
- 1 Thessalonians 4:3-8
- 1 Timothy 2:9-10

The counsel of the entire Word of God is our standard of measurement. These are just a few verses to give us a start. As we see areas in our daily lives that do not line up with the Word, we know we are not free in that area. This should then lead us to the next step.

I – Implore and Petition

Just recognizing an area of bondage will never free us. Once the Holy Spirit has revealed an area to us, the next step is to implore and petition the Father to enable us to cooperate with the finished work of Jesus. We are often tempted to skip this step and take the knowledge of our problem and begin to try to handle it ourselves. We will not gain victory in this way. We will never go free apart from a supernatural work of the Holy Spirit. Write 2 Corinthians 3:17 in the space below.

Every area of bondage that we have is an area excluded from the presence of the Holy Spirit. The above scripture tells us that where the Spirit of the Lord is, there is freedom. Therefore, an area of bondage is an area in which the flesh - sin nature - is reigning, an area not submitted to Christ. It will be the result of one of the roots of sin we discussed earlier. Because of disobedience, ignorance, unbelief, or the sin of another, we have not allowed the Holy Spirit lordship in that area of our lives, and the enemy is capitalizing on it. As we come to understand this, we will see that trying harder is not the way to break out of our bondage; inviting the presence of the Holy Spirit into that area is the way to overcome. When we really grasp this, we will expend our efforts on our knees beseeching the Spirit to come and fill those areas of our lives. We will stop wasting our time trying to do better and begin to cry out for the presence of the Spirit. The Holy Spirit and bondage cannot coexist.

In the example of my relationship with my son, I recognize that I am operating in a lot of fear: fear that he won't make good choices for his life, that he will fall prey to Satan's plans, that our relationship will be estranged, etc. I often take a minor situation and extrapolate his behavior of the moment into some horrible, life debilitating habit. I realize that I am allowing my fear and my son's reaction to situations dictate my responses. Instead of being afraid and reacting to David's behavior, I need to implore the Holy Spirit to give me stability in my emotions and strengthen my faith in His ability to reach my son's heart. I am not allowing the Holy Spirit to reign in the situations I face with David. I keep trying to control them. It was easy to control things when my child was seven; I was bigger than he was ☺. Now that he is growing into a young man, he feels much stronger about things and has a greater desire to get his way. I do not need to give him his way all of the time, but I need to control myself and seek the presence of the Spirit in each and every situation I face with Him. I am aware of this; however, in the heat of the moment, I try to make things go the way I think they should. Instead of continuing to do this, I must grow in my dependency on the Holy Spirit to move on my behalf and for my son as well.

In this case, I might pray, "Father, I feel like I am losing control of my son. I see him doing things that I am afraid might hurt him. I also see that I am not inviting the Spirit to be lord in this situation. Please forgive me for trying to depend on myself. Holy Spirit, I invite you to come and take your rightful place in my mind. I will trust you to preserve my relationship with my son, and I ask you to work in his heart the desire to submit to you and the authority you have established in his life. I ask you to be present and mighty in all my dealings with my son. I praise you and thank you for your faithfulness to me!" I'm feeling better already ☺!

John15:5 states:

> *"I am the vine; you are the branches. If a man remains in me and I in him, he will bear much fruit; apart from me you can do nothing."*

Once we understand the true source of our freedom – the presence of the Holy Spirit - and begin to ask Him to be present, we then move into the next step toward freedom. We will discuss this tomorrow. Hope to see you then!

Day Three

Listen, Obey, Behold the Handiwork of God

Yesterday, we began our discussion of the general path to freedom. We called that path LIBERTY. There are seven general steps we must take if we are to walk out of any bondage. The first two steps were (1) Look and examine, and (2) Implore and petition. We must examine our lives in the light of God's Word and, with the help of the Holy Spirit, we must identify areas of bondage. We must then ask the Holy Spirit to enable us to cooperate with Him as He renews that area of our thinking. In other words, invite His presence into that area. At this point, we move to the next step on our path to freedom.

B – Be Attentive and Listen

As we begin to invite the Holy Spirit to be present in these areas of bondage, He begins to move in. Write 1 Thessalonians 5:24 in the space below.

When the Holy Spirit begins to invade this space, it is often very difficult as he seldom moves into an area without it costing us something. He understands exactly why we are in bondage in a given area, and has to bring us into agreement with God or we will not go free. Therefore we must be attentive to His still, small voice and must learn to listen to the promptings of His will. The more we listen, the better we get at hearing. When we invite the Holy Spirit to get involved, He accepts and begins a liberating work in our lives.

E – Exercise Choice

As the Spirit begins to speak to us in our areas of bondage, we are then faced with a choice. What are we going to do with the information He gives? In order to reach our destination of freedom, we have to decide to do what He tells us. This is really hard, because we're required to change our habits of behavior. Choosing to obey is the blood, sweat, and tears of the freedom process. During this step we learn to cooperate with the Holy Spirit which can be very painful. He gives specific instructions about our issues, and we must choose to obey if we are to progress toward freedom. In the example of my relationship with my son, this would be when the Spirit might bring to my mind scriptures to claim that assure me of God's faithfulness. He might give me a specific instruction addressing David's behavior in a given moment. He might say, "Let this one go, let it slide," or "Nail this one hard; it's got big consequences."

He might prompt me to give David a hug for no reason and tell him how precious he is, or I may be prompted to just keep my mouth shut and let my husband deal with it. You have no idea how much that costs me☺! It is during this step that we say, "Okay, Lord, I am going to do what you say, even though it's not what I want. I believe You know best." During this step, the Spirit reveals the root of sin causing the bondage. He may show us an area of disobedience from which we need to repent, or show us an area of ignorance and lead us to ask for wisdom. He may reveal where we are operating in unbelief so we can cry out, "Help me overcome my unbelief," or he may show us an area of wounding that needs the healing power of His presence. In my case, He has revealed to me an area of unbelief – fear. I now have to choose what to do with this knowledge.

It is this step that requires us to die to ourselves and live unto Christ in the given area. Fill in the blanks to Romans 8:13.

> *"For if you live according to the sinful nature, you will die; but if by*
>
> *the ________ you _____ ____ ________ the misdeeds of the body, you will live,"*

As we listen to His guidance in our daily struggle and respond with agreement, we are putting to death the misdeeds of the body. In doing this, we are cooperating with Him as He leads us to experience the freedom we have been given. As freedom becomes our reality, we are then heading into the next step in the process.

R – Recognize and Regard

As we begin to listen to the Holy Spirit and agree with Him, He begins to set us free. Total freedom may not be immediate, but if we keep on keeping on, He will accomplish it. Slowly but surely we will experience liberty. When this happens, it is so important to recognize the one who deserves credit and honor for our deliverance from bondage. This is when we allow our hearts to become grateful and offer our thanksgiving and praise. As we begin to see freedom in a given area, we need to get excited. Satan wants us to live timidly, but don't do it!!! He will attempt to discourage us and try to convince us that our freedom is temporary. During this season, he will often send others to remind us of our bondage. We have all experienced a time when we were overcoming something, and someone came along and reminded us of what we did or were. This is a tactic of the enemy, but we must be strong! Let our hearts rise in faith, and let us praise our God for He is doing a new work within us!

At this stage we have actually experienced or are experiencing victory, and we need to express our deep gratitude for His faithfulness. The following verses are wonderful examples of praise and thanksgiving to God for his liberating power.

Psalm 18:16-19	Psalm 56:10-13	Psalm 107	Psalm 118:5-7
Psalm 30:1-4	Psalm 68:19-20	Psalm 109:30-31	Psalm 145:13-21
Psalm 34:1-8	Psalm 103:1-5	Psalm 116:1-14	Psalm 150

Remember, Satan will not hang around where God is being exalted. God is faithful and we can trust Him.

Day Four

Defending Your Territory

At this point on our path to freedom, we have examined our lives and allowed the Holy Spirit to reveal to us an area of bondage; we have implored the Holy Spirit to come and be present in this area; we have listened to Him and cooperated with Him; we have experienced freedom in the area; and we have given thanksgiving and praise to God for the work He is doing/has done. Now we are ready for step six.

T – Take our stand

Now is the season that we must take our stand and refuse to give any ground back to the enemy. Gaining freedom over a particular bondage does not mean we will remain free. Maintaining our freedom requires constant vigilance. Christ won for us the ability to live free, but it is up to us to exercise that right and actually experience it. Visualize a country that wins its independence from another. After the war, will the victor's military return home and live in the bliss of freedom? No! They will establish border guards and diligently defend their position. We are no different. Once we gain freedom in a given area, we also have to establish our border guard and diligently defend our position. We can never be lazy and live free. Consequently, this constant vigilance will last for the rest of our lives.

We stay free by standing our ground. Many passages in the Word instruct us regarding this "standing." Often these scriptures use the word "stand," "continue," or "walk in" which are all terms that indicate the same concept . . . stand your ground. Let's examine several. Each scripture gives hints as to how we might accomplish this lifelong task. After reading, record the hint or instruction found in the passage that will enable us to stand our ground.

[emphasis added]

James 1:25

> *"But the man who* ***looks intently*** *into the perfect law that gives freedom, and he* ***continues to do this, not forgetting what he has heard, but doing it****—he will be blessed in what he does."*

Thought: The "perfect law" referred to in this verse is Christ.

Hint: ____

Psalm 119:45

"I will walk about in freedom, for I have ***sought out your precepts****."*

Hint: ____

Galatians 5:1

"It is for freedom that Christ has set us free. Stand firm, then, and ***do not let yourselves*** *be burdened again by a yoke of slavery."*

Hint: ____

Romans 5:1-2

"Therefore, since we have been justified through faith, we have peace with God through our Lord Jesus Christ, 2 through whom we have gained access by faith into this ***grace*** *in which we now stand . . . "*

Hint: ____

Romans 11:20

"Granted. But they were broken off because of unbelief, and you stand by ***faith****. Do not be arrogant, but be afraid."*

Hint: ____

Romans 14:4

"Who are you to judge someone else's servant? To his own master, he stands or falls. And he will stand, for the ***Lord is able*** to make him stand."

Hint: ____

1 Corinthians 10:12

"So, if you think you are standing firm, **be careful** *that you don't fall!"*

Hint: ____

1 Corinthians 15:58

"Therefore, my dear brothers, stand firm. ***Let nothing move you. Always give yourselves fully to the work of the Lord,*** because you know that your labor in the Lord is not in vain."

Hint: ____

1 Corinthians 16:13

*"****Be on your guard****; stand firm in the faith;* ***be men of courage****;* ***be strong****."*

Hint: ____

2 Corinthians 1:21

*"Now it is **God who makes** both us and you stand firm in Christ. He anointed us,"*

Hint: ______________________________

2 Corinthians 1:24

"Not that we lord it over your faith, but we work with you for your joy, because it is by faith you stand firm."

Hint: ______________________________

2 Thessalonians 2:15

*"So then, brothers, stand firm and **hold fast to the teachings** we passed on to you, whether by word of mouth or* by letter."

Hint: ______________________________

1 Peter 5:12

*"With the help of Silas, whom I regard as a faithful brother, I have written to you briefly, encouraging you and testifying that this is the true **grace of God**. **Stand** fast in it."*

Hint: ______________________________

Ephesians 6:10-18

*"Finally, **be strong in the Lord and in his mighty power**. 11 **Put on the full armor of God** so that you can take your stand against the devil's schemes. 12 For our struggle is not against flesh and blood, but against the rulers, against the authorities, against the powers of this dark world and against the spiritual forces of evil in the heavenly realms. 13 Therefore **put on the full armor of God**, so that when the day of evil comes, you may be able to stand your ground, and after you have done everything, to stand. 14 Stand firm then, with the **belt of truth** buckled around your waist, with the **breastplate of righteousness** in place, 15 and with your feet fitted with the readiness that comes from the **gospel of peace**. 16 In addition to all this, take up the **shield of faith**, with which you can extinguish all the flaming arrows of the evil one. 17 Take the **helmet of salvation** and the sword of the Spirit, which is the **word of God**. 18 And **pray in the Spirit** on all occasions with all kinds of prayers and requests . . . "*

Hint: ______________________________

____

____

Following is a list of things I'm sure you wrote on the lines above. These are the things that will enable us to stand our ground upon gaining our freedom.

By placing our faith in God's grace we will be able to:

- Seek to know the heart of God through prayer and reading His Word
- Act upon God's truth as he reveals it. Be doers of the Word.
- Trust that the Lord is able to make us stand.
- Hold fast to the teachings of Christ. Let nothing move us.
- Be steadfast toward the Lord. Give ourselves fully to His Work.
- Be careful and constantly on guard.
- Be courageous and strong.
- Put on the full armor of God.

    1. belt of truth
    2. breastplate of righteousness
    3. helmet of salvation
    4. gospel of peace
    5. shield of faith
    6. sword of the Spirit – the Word of God

By asking the Holy Spirit to work these things in our lives and by depending on Him to do it, we will stand our ground, not allowing the enemy to take us back into bondage once we have been set free.

Allow me to share with you an example of how the enemy might try to take us back into a bondage from which we have been freed. There was a time in my life when I was caught up in the bondage of gossip. As I began to seek the Lord in earnest, I prayed that He would show me the truth about myself and change whatever was in my life that He didn't like. I began to **look** at my life and examine it in light of God's Word. The Holy Spirit did, indeed, highlight certain areas of bondage, and gossip was one of them. I began to **implore** the Holy Spirit to set me free from this, and He revealed to me ways to stop gossiping: praying that He would guard my mouth every time the phone rang; taking each failure to Him immediately and asking for forgiveness and help; telling others I would not gossip; etc. By **being attentive** to His promptings and **exercising my choice** to cooperate with Him, I began to walk out of this bondage until I never gossiped. I **recognized** His work in my life in this area, and it filled my heart with thanksgiving and praise. Gossip wasn't even a temptation to me . . . until recently.

Not long ago, I had an individual with whom I spent quite a bit of time. For some reason, every time I got together with her, things would come up about other people, and I found myself edging back toward gossip. I lost my peace when I spent time with her. There came a period of a few days when I felt a distinct absence of fellowship with the Holy Spirit. I began to pray in earnest and ask Him what the problem was, and He revealed to me that I was letting my guard down in this area of gossip. He asked me if I really wanted to go back to that again. I, of course, said "No Way!" and asked Him what I should do about the situation. I didn't want to wound this precious friend or project my sin upon her. The Spirit led me to tell her that she needed to treat me just as she would a recovering alcoholic. In the same way that she wouldn't consider drinking in front of me if I were an alcoholic, I asked her not to consider talking about anyone with me because I was a recovered "gossip-aholic." I simply told her that I did not want to go back to where I had been. This took courage, but my friend was extremely supportive and our relationship is better than ever. I **took my stand.** This is an example of how, by God's grace, we work with the Holy Spirit to guard our territory of victory. Every situation will be different, but the principles will always be the same. This is how, when we have done everything, we stand (Ephesians 6:13). We stand by His wonderful grace through faith and obedience. This standing will lead us into the final step in our path to freedom. We will discuss this step in the next lesson.

Day Five

The Harvest

So, here we are. We have reached our goal of freedom, and are standing firm defending our territory. Regarding our bondage, we are free from external control, free to exercise our choice, free to participate in the rights and privileges of citizenship in the kingdom of God, and free from anything that would set itself up against the knowledge and the Word of God. Now we are ready for the fun part!

Y – Yield our crops

In this step, we begin to yield our crops. The evidence of freedom will be displayed in our lives. There may be other areas of bondage with which we will contend, but in this area, we are free. Now we begin to reap a harvest from the seeds of obedience we have sown. Many verses in the Bible speak of this season of harvest. Sometimes they refer to this harvest as "producing a crop," "reaping," or "yielding." Each phrasing is referring to that season in our lives when we get to partake of the returns of our labors. We have agreed with God, and, through faith, our freedom in Christ has become our reality.

Read the following verses and write the promise of harvest found in each. The first one is done for you.

Matthew 13:23

> **Promise:** If I hear the Word and understand it, I will produce a crop, yielding a hundred, sixty, or thirty times what was sown.

Luke 8:15

> **Promise:** ____
>
> ____

John 12:24

> **Promise:** ____
>
> ____

James 3:18

Promise: ____

____

Galatians 6:7-9

Promise: ____

____

Romans 6:22

Promise: ____

____

2 Corinthians 9:10

Promise: ____

____

Hebrews 12:11

Promise: ____

____

When we agree with God and obey Him, we will go free. A life of freedom reflects God's glory. The glory of God is attractive and will draw others to us. We, in turn, can point them to Jesus. **This is the essence of ministry.** God does a wonderful work in our lives; it shows; others ask how we experienced "it"; and we tell them. This process will take on many faces, but the principle will be the same. All true ministry stems from our own personal relationship and experience with our God. For this reason, if we do not personally walk the path of freedom, we will never be able to show others the way. But if we will pay the price of walking that path, oh, the blessed season of harvest!

Before we close this discussion on yielding our crops, I want to revisit a question raised earlier. Its answer is an important key in this final step of the freedom process. The question asked related to the concept that Jesus came to free us from external control. In freeing us from external control, He enabled us to be self-controlled. The question was asked, "What do we do with our control?" The answer: we use it to determine who will be our master. The Word of God says that we are slaves to whatever has mastered us (2 Peter 2:19). When we partake of the freedom Christ provided, nothing is mastering us. Look at what Paul says in 1 Corinthians 6:12.

> *"'Everything is permissible for me'—but not everything is beneficial.*
> *'Everything is permissible for me'—but I will not be mastered by anything."*

In other verses, Paul tells us to become slaves to God and to righteousness (Romans 6:22, Romans 6:18). So how does this come together? On the one hand, we are told we are free and God does not want to control us. On the other hand, we are supposed to be slaves to God and righteousness.

The answer to this quandary is found in the following passages. [emphasis added]

1 Corinthians 9:19

> *"Though I am free and belong to no man,* ***I make myself*** *a slave to everyone, to win as many as possible."*

Romans 6:19

> *"I put this in human terms because you are weak in your natural selves. Just as* ***you*** *used to* ***offer*** *the parts of your body in slavery to impurity and to ever-increasing wickedness, so now* ***offer*** *them in slavery to righteousness leading to holiness."*

Galatians 5:13

> *"You, my brothers, were called to be free. But* ***do not use your freedom to indulge the sinful nature; rather, serve*** *one another in love."*

1 Peter 2:16

> *"Live as free men, but do not use your freedom as a cover-up for evil; live as servants of God.*

Please read Romans chapter six in its entirety.

In order to live in freedom and yield a crop for the kingdom, we must choose to obey God. God will not make us obey Him, but if we choose not to live a life of obedience, we will walk back into bondage. I said earlier that we will not automatically stay free, but must choose to stay free. Paul said that he belonged to no man, but he chose to make himself a slave. This is the key to a great harvest. Look at what an effective life he lived! He is still affecting lives all over the world! When we choose to submit ourselves to God, we will experience a life that we cannot even comprehend. Our ministries will grow, and our "death to self" will produce abundant life in the world around us.

What do we do with our freedom? We choose to give it to God. Then we reap a harvest that cannot be measured. When we place what is ours in the hands of God, it becomes so much more. When we choose to die to self, it is then that we truly live. As we live in the freedom we have been given, our lives will yield a crop thirty, sixty, or a hundred times over. This is what I want! I want to yield as big a crop as I possibly can, for this is the only everlasting yield we have. Everything else will be nothing when we leave this earth, but this increase will meet us in eternity.

LIBERTY! Wow! I had no idea this lesson would be so lengthy. Our discussion of freedom, what it is, and how to make it our reality, has been a long and maybe tedious journey. However, I pray that its truth will bear much fruit in our lives. Our belief about freedom will have a major impact not only on our own lives but on countless others as well. We need to believe rightly about freedom and how to live in it. I pray that the Holy Spirit will enable each of us to live in the freedom that is ours and to produce an abundant crop for the kingdom of God! Thank you, Jesus, for making this possible!

From my Heart to Yours

- *CONCLUSION* -

Dear sisters, It is hard to believe we have reached the end of this journey together. Who knows, maybe there will be a "So, What's the Deal? Part Two" ☺. My heart's desire is for each of us to become the strong women of God that He intends for us to be. I want us to change the world in our generation. If I deal victoriously in my life and cover the territory that God has given me and you do the same with what has been given you, we will accomplish this! I want us to realize that we serve a big God! I want us to see Him as He truly is, not as an uninterested, hard to touch being, way off somewhere. He is an abiding, living presence with a heart that can be touched! He really cares about the details, and He really cares about what we do with Him. We matter to Him!

Do not let this be the end of your "journey" to delve deeper into the Word and a relationship with Christ. Trust Him to work these truths into your very soul so that you may have life abundantly (John 10:10 NAS) and reflect the glory of God! My greatest desire for this study is that it would cultivate the same passionate love for God, His Word, His Son, and His children that has grown in my heart as I have experienced the truths we have studied. May God bless your continued journey and may you live free!

With this in mind, we constantly pray for you, that our God may count you worthy of his calling, and that by his power he may fulfill every good purpose of yours and every act prompted by your faith.

- 2 Thessalonians 1:11

Love in Christ, Sharon

Bibliography

(1) Luther, Martin, and John Nicholas Lenker. *The Complete Sermons of Martin Luther.* Vol. 1. Grand Rapids, MI: Baker, 2000. Print.

All scripture references unless otherwise noted were taken from the HOLY BIBLE, NEW INTERNATIONAL VERSION. Copyright © 1973, 1978, 1984 by International Bible Society. Used by permission of Zondervan. All rights reserved.

Scripture quotations marked NAS are from *New American Standard Bible. © Copyright 1960, 1962, 1963, 1968, 1971, 1972, 1973, 1975, 1977, 1995 by Lockman Foundation. © Copyright 1999 by The Zondervan Corporation.* Grand Rapids, Michigan

Strong, James. *Strong's Concordance of the Bible.* Nashville: T. Nelson, 1980. Print.

The American Heritage Dictionary of the English Language, New College Edition
© Copyright 1969, 1970, 1971, 1973, 1975, 1976 by Houghton Mifflin Company

Dictionary.com Unabridged. Random House Dictionary, Random House, Inc. 16 Aug. 2010. <Dictionary.com http://dictionary.reference.com/browse/truth>.

LISTENING GUIDES

Week One

1. God is ________ in ______.

- __________
- __________
- __________

2. Man is made in the image of God.

- Man has a _________, ________, and _________.

3. At salvation, our ________ are one with God's ________.

4. Our minds then receive the ability to know the thoughts of God, but they do not automatically do so. Therefore we must undergo a process called ____________ _____ ___________.

5. If we want the truths of the Bible to become realities in our lives, we must learn to ____________ ________ ________.

6. What we ___________ determines the ___________ we make which determines our _____________ _____________.

7. Every choice made in accordance with the _________ ultimately leads to ___________ and ___________________!

8. We must learn to make choices based on the ___________, not the _________.

"So God created man
in his own image, in the
image of God he
created him; male and
female he created them."

- Genesis 1:27

Week Two

- The power of God is real and available to every ____________________!

- That power is accessed by _______________.

- Our faith does not rest on ___________ ________________, but

  on ________ _______ __________ _________!

- Jesus came so that we could live ______________, and He wants us filled with His power and ability.

  1 Corinthians 2:1-5, Matthew 3:11

- Do we realize that the power of God truly lives within us?

- We so often do not live as if we do. We are often filled with fear, insecurity, strife, and lack of peace because we do not place our faith in God and His ability to do what He says.

  Romans 4:20-21, Romans 8:11, 1 Corinthians 6:14, 2 Timothy 1:7-10

- We often talk far beyond our _______________________.

  1 Corinthians 4:20

- God has given us ________________________ we need to live the reality of His Word.

  2 Peter 1:3

- This is our ___________________! This is what we were made for.

- One reason we don't do this is we continually try to live supernaturally

  in our ________ ___________________.

• Our ability to live beyond ourselves, to be overcomers, lies in our ability to live in total _________________ on God through Christ. It is His strength that accomplishes all things.

• Apart from Him we _______ ________ _________________.

John 15:5, 2 Corinthians 12:9, 2 Corinthians 13:3-4, Ephesians 3:20, Colossians 1:29

• How does what we see in the Word become our reality and enable us to affect those around us?

____

____

____

____

____

• God has called us to the great and wonderful privilege of reflecting the truth of Him to the world around us.

• We cannot give away what we don't have.

• Oh that we would have this revelation, that we would believe Him to be who He says that He is! If we don't, who will!

• We are the ________ ____ ___________! We are meant to reflect God in our generation!

• How I pray that we do!

Ephesians 1:17-21, Philippians 3:10-11, Ephesians 6:10

Week Three

Learning to hear God's voice.

1. ______________________________

Psalm 50:1, Proverbs 8:1-4, Isaiah 48:17-18, Isaiah 65:1-2

2. ______________________________

Isaiah 66:4, Psalm 119:36-37, Psalm 119:72, Psalm 119:81, Psalm 84:10

3. ______________________________

Leviticus 19:31, Deuteronomy 4:29, 1 Chronicles 16:11,
2 Chronicles 12:14, Psalm 10:4, Psalm 14:2, Psalm 34:10,
Proverbs 28:5, Amos 5:4, Acts 17:27, Hebrews 11:6

4. ______________________________

Deuteronomy 8:3, Hosea 4:6, Psalm 119:105, Matthew 24:35,
John 8:32, John 15:7, John 17:17, Romans 10:17, Ephesians 6:17,
2 Timothy 2:15, Hebrews 4:12

5. ______________________________

Matthew 7:7-8, Mark 11:24, John 15:7, Romans 12:12, Colossians 4:2, James 1:5,
James 4:2-3, 1 Peter 4:7, 1 John 5:14-15, Revelation 5:8

6. ______________________________

1 Samuel 15:22, Psalm 81:11, Proverbs 3:5-6, Luke 11:28, Romans 10:3,
Romans 12:2, 2 Corinthians 10:5, 2 Timothy 4:3, Hebrews 5:7, Hebrews 12:9

"The Mighty One, God,
the Lord, speaks and
summons the earth from
the rising of the sun
to where it sets."

- Psalm 50:1

Week Four

- God has created a void within the heart of every human being.

  Ecclesiastes 3:11, 2 Corinthians 5:2-4, Hebrews 11:16

- He wants to fill that void with _________________.

  Psalm 145:16, Isaiah 55:2, Isaiah 58:11, John 4:13-14, Jeremiah 31:14, John 10:10

- When we encounter voids, we have a tendency to try to fill them.
- We don't like voids. We like ________________ and ________________.
- Filling _______________ never fills our _______ ________.
- Satan tempts us to fill voids with things _____ _____ _______, and it only causes _______ _______.
- Does God care about our voids?
- God not only cares about our voids, He ________________ ______________ them.
- His purpose for this is to form a ______________ _________________ upon Him.
- He wants us to know that He is our __________ _____________!
- God wants to prepare us to handle _______ fullness ___________.
- He wants us _______ _____ __________________.
- But He wants us full and overflowing with _______ _______, not our _______.

  Luke 11:13

- God really is about fullness, but He is about ___________ ____________.

- If our fullness stops with ____, it isn't directed fullness.
- God desires that we have an overabundance of comfort, provision, wisdom, peace, etc., not just so we can have them, but that we share them and help others form a relationship with Jesus.
- God will allow us to experience voids for the purpose of drawing us into a greater _______________and ______________ with Him.
- He allows the void to cause us to ____________ Him more that He might become our _____ ____ ____, that He might _____ ______ with the power of His Holy Spirit, that we will go forth and ________ ______ _______ ___ ____ to our world.
- When we are facing a void in our lives, let us embrace it as God's call to ________ __________ to His heart.
- He cares and He is intentionally positioning us to receive His best!
- Sometimes we have to be willing to experience voids for a season in order to receive the abundance from God.
- Are we willing to wait on the Lord?
- Are we willing to refuse comfort and provision from any other hand but our God's?
- We must learn to wait on the Lord.

  Psalm 5:3, Psalm 27:14, Psalm 40:1, Isaiah 26:8, Isaiah 64:4, Proverbs 8:34

- Let's close this session with a final thought.

  Jeremiah 2:13

- May we neither forsake ______ _________ _____ _________ _________ nor ______ _______ _______ ___________!
- Let us wait on the Lord and see what wonderful things He has in store!

Week Five

- Every Christian prays, but does every Christian pray ____________?
- God desires to move on our behalf. He desires to show Himself __________!

  James 5:16, 2 Thessalonians 1:11, John 14:12-14

- Since this is so, why don't we pray with ________________ and in ________________?
  - o Failure to ______________God's Word.
  - o Failure to believe God cares about the ___________.
  - o Lack of _________________.
  - o Lack of ____________ in God and our relationship with Him.
- Failure to believe God's Word _______ _________ _________.

  Matthew 13:58, Numbers 14:20-24, Hebrews 3:19

- The primary thing that God wants from us is our __________.

  Hebrews 11:6

- We will not pray about things that we don't think God cares about.
- Many Christians believe God only cares about the ________ things.
- Who gets to define what things are big?
- It all matters to God, because _______ matter to God.

  1 Peter 5:7, Philippians 4:4-7

- Prayer is an expression of _______ and __________.
- Scripture tells us God cares about our details.

  Luke 12:6-7, Luke 12:22-34

- There is a direct correlation between answered prayer and _____________.

  John 15:7, 1 John 5:14

- Abiding in Christ results in __________ ______, which leads

  to ________ ___________!

- God wants to answer prayer. He wants us to see Him as He is.

- But, it has to be _______ way, not ________.

  Isaiah 30:18, John 15:8

- God hears our prayers and continually watches over us. We have to know this!

  Deuteronomy 11:12, Psalm 121:4, Psalm 34:15, 1 John 5:15

- Our righteousness is not based on performance, rather on the finished

  work of ________ _________.

  Galatians 2:20-21, 1 John 3:21-23, Hebrews 4:14-16

- There is a connection between our ____________ before God

  and our _______________ to pray.

- God is the God of our entire lives – every detail.

- Pray about everything, submit to God, wait on Him, and Trust Him!

  Proverbs 3:5-6

- Let's close by reading Ephesians 3:20-21.

  "Now to him who is able to do immeasurably more than all we ask or imagine, according to his power that is at work within us, 21 to Him be glory in the church and in Christ Jesus throughout all generations, for ever and ever! Amen."

Week Six

Who do you say I am?

Matthew 16:13-16

God knows the plans that He has for us, and He knows that in order to accomplish them, we must _________ who He is!

His plans are so far beyond us that in order to accomplish them we will have to depend on the _________ ___ ________ through Christ.

John 15:5-8

God's purpose for man hasn't changed since the beginning of time.

From the beginning, God has been creating a group of people to _______ _______ _______.

Exodus 19:6, 2 Samuel 7:23, Titus 2:14, Revelation 21:3, Revelation 1:5-6

God is the one who is doing this, but He needs us to _________ ________.

- To believe that He _____ who He says that He is.

  Exodus 3:14, John 8:58, John 14:6, John 6:35, John 8:12, Ephesians 1:19-23, 1 Timothy 6:15

- To believe what He says.

  Romans 4:20-21

What are some of the things that He says?

1. ________ ________ ________

   Galatians 5:1, 2 Corinthians 3:17, Isaiah 42:7

2. ________ ________ ________

   Hebrews 13:5, Matthew 28:20

3. ________ ________ ________ ________

   Acts 1:8, Ephesians 1:18-19, Ephesians 3:20, Colossians 1:10-11

4. ________ ________ ________ ________ ________ ________

   John 10:10

5. ________ ________ ________

   Acts 1:10-11, John 14:1-3

6. ________ ________ ________ ________ ________ ________ ________

   Jeremiah 29:11, 1 Corinthians 2:9

7. ________ ________ ________ ________– **we need not fear death.**

   John 6:58, John 11:25, 1 Thessalonians 5:10, 1 Thessalonians 4:17

8. ________ ________ ________ ________ ________ ________ ________

   Isaiah 54:17 (NKJV)

9. ________ ________ ________ ________

   Luke 10:19

10. ________ ________ ________ ________ ________

    Romans 8:37

11. ________ ________ ________ ________

    Romans 8:1

12. ________ ________ ________ ________ ________ ________

    Romans 8:28

13. ______ ________ ___ and ____________ ______ ___________ ______ _______

______ _______

Romans 8:38-39, 1 John 3:1

14. _____ ________ __________ ________ _____ _______

Galatians 6:7-9

15. ___ _____ __________ ___________, ___ _____ _______ ___ ___

1 Peter 5:6

16. _____ ______ _____ ____________ ___ _____ _________ _______

John 15:18-21, Matthew 24:9

17. _____ ______ _______ ___ ___________ _____ _______ ________

Matthew 12:36

18. ___ _____ _______ _______ ___ ____________ _____ __ ________

2 Corinthians 5:10

Do we believe God to the extent that we are changed?

This is the challenge before us.

Who do we say that He is as is evidenced in the privacy of our own hearts and homes?

Who do we say that He is as is evidenced in the reality of our lives?

Dear Sisters, we serve a mighty God.

> **Romans 4:17**, *"As it is written: 'I have made you a father of many nations.' He is our father in the sight of God, in whom he believed – the God who gives life to the dead and calls things that are not as though they were."*

This is who He is! But who do you say that He is?

"I am the vine; you are
the branches. If a man remains
in me and I in him, he will
bear much fruit; apart from me
you can do nothing"

- John 15:5

Week Seven

- The Great Commission

  Matthew 28:18-20

- We have been _____________ with the gospel.

  1 Corinthians 4:1-2, 1Timothy 1:11-12, 1Timothy 6:20

- The Gospel will always _________ ______ ________ _____ ______!

- If the gospel is not displaying the truth of God in our lives, then we deceive ourselves.

  James 1:22-25

- Just receiving truth does not make it a reality in our lives.

- _____________ it to the extent that it __________ ______ ________ is what counts.

- We can't give away what we don't have.

- Am I promoting a works-oriented salvation? No!

- I am promoting a _________ -oriented life.

  John 6:28-29, Galatians 3:1-5, Ephesians 2:10, Philippians 2:13

- We were meant to make a difference in our generation!

- But not just with ________, but in _________!

  Colossians 4:5, 1Timothy 4:15-16, Philippians 2:15-16

• The idea is:

1. God puts things before us.

   John 9:3

2. He wants us to trust Him so that He can __________ ____________ to us.

3. We behold ______ _______________!

4. We ___________ His awesomeness!

   Deuteronomy 3:24

• We ___________ with God in the great commission.

2 Corinthians 6:1

• We are meant to live a life of _________.

• God's people have always been called to do so.

Hebrews 11:1 – 12:3

Made in the USA
Monee, IL
24 January 2024